Social Commentators

GREAT ARTISTS OF THE WESTERN WORLD

Social Commentators

William Hogarth

Gustave Courbet

Henri de Toulouse-Lautrec

Diego Rivera

MARSHALL CAVENDISH · LONDON · NEW YORK · SYDNEY

Staff Credits

Editors	Clive Gregory LLB Sue Lyon BA (Honours)	**Picture Researchers**	Vanessa Fletcher BA (Honours) Flavia Howard BA (Honours) Jessica Johnson BA
Art Editors	Chris Legee BFA Kate Sprawson BA (Honours) Keith Vollans LSIAD	**Production Controllers**	Tom Helsby Alan Stewart BSc
Deputy Editor	John Kirkwood BSc (Honours)	**Secretary**	Lynn Smail
Sub-editors	Caroline Bugler BA (Honours), MA Sue Churchill BA (Honours) Alison Cole BA, MPhil Jenny Mohammadi Nigel Rodgers BA (Honours), MA Penny Smith Will Steeds BA (Honours), MA	**Editorial Director** **Publishing Manager** **Managing Editor**	Maggi McCormick Robert Paulley BSc Alan Ross BA (Honours)
Designers	Stuart John Julie Stanniland	**Consultant and Authenticator**	Sharon Fermor BA (Honours) Lecturer in the Extra-Mural Department of London University and Lecturer in Art History at Sussex University

Reference Edition Published 1988

Published by Marshall Cavendish Corporation
147 West Merrick Road
Freeport, Long Island
N.Y. 11520

Typeset by Litho Link Ltd., Welshpool
Printed and Bound by Dai Nippon
Printing Co., Hong Kong Ltd.

Library of Congress Cataloging-in-Publication Data

Main entry under title:

Great Artists of the Western World II.

Includes index.
1. Artists – Biography. I. Marshall Cavendish
Corporation.
N40.G774 1988   709'.2'2 [B]   88–4317
ISBN 0–86307–900–8 (set)

ISBN 0–86307–900–8 (set)
       0–86307–761–7 (vol)

Preface

Looking at pictures can be one of the greatest pleasures that life has to offer. Note, however, those two words 'can be'; all too many of us remember all too clearly those grim afternoons of childhood when we were dragged, bored to tears and complaining bitterly, through room after room of Italian primitives by well-meaning relations or tight-lipped teachers. It was enough to put one off pictures for life – which, for some of us, was exactly what it did.

For if gallery-going is to be the fun it should be, certain conditions must be fulfilled. First, the pictures we are to see must be good pictures. Not necessarily great pictures – even a few of these can be daunting, while too many at a time may prove dangerously indigestible. But they must be well-painted, by good artists who know precisely both the effect they want to achieve and how best to achieve it. Second, we must limit ourselves as to quantity. Three rooms – four at the most – of the average gallery are more than enough for one day, and for best results we should always leave while we are still fresh, well before satiety sets in. Now I am well aware that this is a counsel of perfection: sometimes, in the case of a visiting exhibition or, perhaps, when we are in a foreign city with only a day to spare, we shall have no choice but to grit our teeth and stagger on to the end. But we shall not enjoy ourselves quite so much, nor will the pictures remain so long or so clearly in our memory.

The third condition is all-important: we must know something about the painters whose work we are looking at. And this is where this magnificent series of volumes – one of which you now hold in your hands – can make all the difference. No painting is an island: it must, if it is to be worth a moment's attention, express something of the personality of its painter. And that painter, however individual a genius, cannot but reflect the country, style and period, together with the views and attitudes of the people among whom he or she was born and bred. Even a superficial understanding of these things will illuminate a painting for us far better than any number of spotlights, and if in addition we have learnt something about the artist as a person – life and loves, character and beliefs, friends and patrons, and the places to which he or she travelled – the interest and pleasure that the work will give us will be multiplied a hundredfold.

Great Artists of the Western World will provide you with just such an insight into the life

and work of some of the outstanding painters of Europe and America. The text is informative without ever becoming dry or academic, not limiting itself to the usual potted biographies but forever branching out into the contemporary world outside and beyond workshop or studio. The illustrations, in colour throughout, have been dispensed in almost reckless profusion. For those who, like me, revel in playing the Attribution Game – the object of which is to guess the painter of each picture before allowing one's eye to drop to the label – the little sections on 'Trademarks' are a particularly happy feature; but every aficionado will have particular preferences, and I doubt whether there is an art historian alive, however distinguished, who would not find some fascinating nugget of previously unknown information among the pages that follow.

This series, however, is not intended for art historians. It is designed for ordinary people like you and me – and for our older children – who are fully aware that the art galleries of the world constitute a virtually bottomless mine of potential enjoyment, and who are determined to extract as much benefit and advantage from it as they possibly can. All the volumes in this collection will enable us to do just that, expanding our knowledge not only of art itself but also of history, religion, mythology, philosophy, fashion, interior decoration, social customs and a thousand other subjects as well. So let us not simply leave them around, flipping idly through a few of their pages once in a while. Let us read them as they deserve to be read – and welcome a new dimension in our lives.

John Julius Norwich is a writer and broadcaster who has written histories of Venice and of Norman Sicily as well as several works on history, art and architecture. He has also made over twenty documentary films for television, including the recent Treasure Houses of Britain series which was widely acclaimed after repeated showings in the United States.

Lord Norwich is Chairman of the Venice in Peril Fund, and member of the Executive Committee of the British National Trust, an independently funded body established for the protection of places of historic interest and natural beauty.

John Julius Norwich

Contents

Introduction

The nature of the relationship between an artist and the society in which he or she works is a pivotal question, and one that lies at the heart of developments in Western art. Succeeding generations of painters have debated as to whether they should place their talents at the service of the public or whether they should pursue their own, individual visions, irrespective of the value this might have to society at large.

Initially, the balance certainly lay in favour of service. Medieval artists were given the status of craftsmen, which meant that, while technical ability was highly prized, inspiration and personal expression were neither expected nor encouraged. In religious commissions, an explicit, iconographical programme was frequently provided for the artist to follow. Under secular patrons, there was usually a degree of freedom, although even a painter of Van Eyck's stature was

Portraits (opposite from left to right): Tate Gallery, London/E. T. Archive; Musée Fabre, Montpellier/Giraudon. This page (from left to right): Musée des Augustins, Toulouse/Photographie Jean Dieuzaide; Gisèle Freund/The John Hillelson Agency

obliged to decorate shields and colour sculptures.

As artists gained financial independence, this element of service was transmuted into a hieratic scale of values, governed by prestige. When the great Academies were founded in the 17th and 18th centuries, they established different categories of painting, which were defined by the quality of their moral purpose. 'High art' was limited to 'history' painting – a term which did not so much describe the subject matter (it also embraced religious and mythological painting), but which required an elevated moral or intellectual aim on the part of the artist. 'Low art', by contrast, referred to those categories, such as landscape, which were designed for pleasure rather than for didactic purpose.

These artificial divisions caused considerable problems for artists. The importance attached to history painting resulted in the creation of many pompous and overblown works and, by the same token, the prejudice against 'low art' cast an unnecessary slur over those art forms that were best equipped to reach a wider public.

Cautionary Tales
This dilemma was already evident in the career of Hogarth. On the one hand, he was passionately committed to the principle of an Academy which would promote a national, English school of painting (the Royal Academy was not founded until 1768) and his ambition, certainly, was to become a history painter, even though his essays in this field (for example, the murals at St Bartholomew's Hospital on p. 16) show that he was patently unsuited to this style. Yet, at the same time, his talents lay precisely in those areas that he and his contemporaries so undervalued.

Hogarth's most memorable paintings were those in which he gave the greatest rein to his naturalism, for example, in his informal portraits (pp.18-19). However, his finest overall achievements were transmitted through the medium of engraving. Hogarth's cautionary tales of A Rake's Progress (pp.24-5) and Marriage à la Mode (pp.30-31) were the pictorial equivalent of the satirical novels of Fielding, Swift and Defoe and, like written works, their success lay in their mass circulation, rather than through being viewed conventionally, as paintings in a gallery.

In this sense, Hogarth's most important contribution to popular art was his campaign for the Copyright Act (known colloquially at the time

as 'Hogarth's Act'), which prohibited the copying of any original image until fourteen years had elapsed. This enabled skilled artists, who did not choose to work in the exalted realms of history painting, to make a respectable living.

Hogarth's preferred subject-matter was the depiction of social and moral ills. However, prints were also a popular medium for the portrayal of political themes. The reasons for this were twofold. Firstly, a printed image could reach a much wider following and, secondly, the immediate but ephemeral issues of politics are incompatible with the enduring medium of painting.

Artistic Freedom
There are, of course, exceptions. David's Oath of the Horatii provides a timeless call to arms, while Picasso's Guernica constitutes an undying image of innocent suffering. However, an impartial observer would probably find it much harder to understand how Courbet's Burial at Ornans (pp. 56-7) or Millet's rather romanticized peasants (p. 53) could have seemed so politically threatening to the society of their time. In fact, this 'threat'

The artists
(opposite, left to right)
Hogarth in a self-portrait,
The Painter and his Pug;
Courbet aged about 30 in a self-portrait.
(below, left to right)
Toulouse-Lautrec in Paris aged 19, in a portrait by his friend, Henri Rachou;
Rivera in a photograph taken in 1952.

The servant of the people
(opposite) Diego Rivera used fresco as the best way to further his aim of bringing art to a mass audience. And here, he shows himself (seated in the centre holding a paintbrush) not as an inspired genius remote from his audience, but as a labourer working in front of and on behalf of the people.

existed largely in the collective mind of the authorities and this sort of governmental paranoia has been echoed more recently by the Nazis, who condemned the work of progressive artists such as Beckmann, Grosz and Dix by exhibiting their pictures in an exhibition of 'Degenerate' art (1937). Not surprisingly, the reputations of these artists have long outlived those of their Hitlerian counterparts.

In the case of Courbet, the real struggle was for artistic liberty. His monumental depictions of peasants and his unsightly bathers were, first and foremost, a challenge to Academic standards of order and beauty. Indeed, his most famous work, The Painter's Studio (pp. 60-61) was a deliberate perversion of the ideals of history painting. For, instead of employing his allegory to preach some elevated, moral message, Courbet used it to glorify the role of the painter. In this way, far from devoting his skills to a populist cause, he was liberating the artist from all duties save those to himself.

This movement towards artistic independence had been gathering pace throughout the 19th century. It originated in the 'art for art' theories put forward by certain Romantic writers, who recognized art as an autonomous entity, free from the restraints of the physical world and its attendant morality, and it culminated in the Aestheticism favoured by some Symbolist painters. This was no 'ivory tower' trend, however, since it enabled artists to explore new frontiers – among them the workings of perception and the human psyche – and, as such, it has proved a significant force in 20th century art.

The Art of the Poster
Inevitably, though, this apparently self-indulgent approach met with stern resistance. One response was provided by William Morris, whose Arts and Crafts movement signalled an attempt to turn back the clock and reorganize painting along the lines of the medieval guild system.

For most socially minded artists, however, the natural response was to gravitate away from easel painting. Toulouse-Lautrec, for example, found a new outlet in posters. This comparatively new medium had benefited enormously from the advances made in colour lithography during the 1860s, and its directness rapidly helped establish it as the 'art gallery of the streets'.

In this regard, Lautrec might be described as an heir to the tradition of Hogarth, even though his works contained no social or political message. For,

despite his blend of unsparing realism and caricature, which was reminiscent of Hogarth's style and, even more so, of the 'ugly realism' to be produced a generation later by the Neue Sachlichkeit (New Objectivity) painters, no moral criticism was intended. Rather, Lautrec's pictures were created as an affectionate tribute to the colourful demi-monde in which he lived.

The Property of the People
An alternative vehicle for public art was provided by the revival of mural-painting. The Norwegian artist, Edvard Munch, had voiced a popular sentiment when he regretted that pictures should 'disappear like a piece of paper' inside a rich man's house, where few could enjoy them. With frescoes, however, 'art will become the property of the people – the work of art will belong to us all'.

This socialist attitude was echoed in the post-Revolutionary communities of Russia and Mexico. The former, however, was embarrassed by its own artistic avant-garde (namely the Constructivist and Suprematist movements) which, despite its support for the Revolution, was deemed to be an elitist legacy of the old order. Initially, these artists were coaxed into utilitarian projects, such as industrial design, before being discarded in favour of the pallid Socialist Realism style.

Rivera visited Moscow in 1927-8 and made contact with the Octobre group, who steered a middle course between the avant-garde and the propagandists. In the event, Octobre were dissolved by Stalin in 1932, but their theories were assimilated by Rivera.

Ironically, some of the Mexican's finest exercises in community painting were produced in the capitalist environment of the United States. In his schemes at Detroit (pp.126-7) and San Francisco (p.8) in particular, Rivera created a harmonious vision of workers, technicians and managers united democratically in the act of labour.

Rivera's work influenced a generation of American artists, most notably Thomas Hart Benton and the 'New Deal' muralists, but his impact on mainstream artistic developments was minimal. In this respect, little has changed since the days of Hogarth. There are still artists who may wish to promote themselves as the conscience of society but, for the most part, they have found other, more immediately effective means for this than easel painting.

Wᵐ Hogarth

1697- 1764

One of Britain's most gifted and influential artists, Hogarth achieved fame both as a painter and as an engraver. His pictures were widely circulated in printed form, and were enormously popular. Their subject matter was drawn from the London the artist observed around him, and his early experience of his father's imprisonment for debt gave him an enduring interest in the seamier sides of life in the city.

Hogarth was working at a time when British art was largely dominated by foreign artists, and he did much to promote the position of native British artists. He also brought fresh vigour to conventional portraiture, and helped introduce theatre pictures and conversation pieces to British art. But it is as the inventor of that particularly British genre – the modern moral narrative – that he is best remembered today.

A Fervent Patriot

Pugnacious and patriotic when it came to recognizing the worth of English art, Hogarth's successful career was a never-ending battle against 'connoisseurs', printsellers and publishing pirates.

William Hogarth was born on 10 November 1697, in Smithfield. His father, Richard Hogarth, was a failed schoolmaster and writer who tried to recoup his fortunes by keeping a superior kind of coffee house for the learned, a place where 'the master of the House, in the absence of others, is always ready to entertain gentlemen in the Latin tongue'. This venture failed, and by the time William was 12, the family was living in the Fleet, a debtors' prison. His mother was making what she could by selling an ointment 'which, in the very moment of application, cures the gripes in young children and prevents fits'. Unfortunately two of her own children, William's brothers, died during this time.

In September 1712, Hogarth's father was released from the Fleet, and the family took up residence in Long Lane. And, just over a year later, with the help of his uncle, Edmund Hogarth, a prosperous victualler at London Bridge, William was apprenticed for seven years to Ellis Gamble, a silver plate engraver.

In the spring of 1720, when his apprenticeship still had nearly one year to run, Hogarth set up on his own. It was a bold gesture, but perhaps a necessary one. His father was dead – worn out, he insisted, by 'the cruel treatment he met with from booksellers and printers'. Uncle Edmund was also dead and had turned against Hogarth's mother and cut her out of his will, so it may well have been essential for William to cut short his apprenticeship and become the breadwinner of the family. This he did by issuing a shop card and opening a business at his mother's house in Long Lane. On the card were printed the words 'W. Hogarth, Engraver' flanked by two figures symbolizing Art and History, making it clear that the young Hogarth would no longer be a mere craftsman but was determined to be an artist – and a history artist at that.

Convinced as he was that the status of English painting should be elevated, Hogarth still found that when he started learning to paint formally in

A London lad
(above) Born and brought up in London, Hogarth spent the first 12 years of his life in Smithfield – an area which had escaped the Great Fire of 1666.

Public introduction
(below) Hogarth, the most English of artists, chose the 23 April for his public debut as it was both St. George's Day and Shakespeare's birthday.

Drama in oils
(right) Hogarth's venture into oil painting proved a success. He painted six versions of The Beggar's Opera, each capturing the drama of the theatre.

British Museum

Sir James Thornhill/Royal Naval College, Greenwich

1720, he had to go to an academy in St Martin's Lane run by two painters of foreign extraction, John Vanderbank and Louis Chéron – and pay a fee of two guineas. Three years later, however, the academy closed, but a free academy was opened by Sir John Thornhill at his house in Covent Garden. Hogarth was one of Thornhill's first pupils, being a great admirer of the history painter who was the first English-born painter to receive a knighthood.

INFORMAL TRAINING

Later, in 1735, when Hogarth's reputation was well established, he founded a 'new' St Martin's Lane Academy, a relatively informal school for practising artists as well as younger students, organized on democratic lines. His attitude to academies or schools of art was to remain ambivalent. While appreciating the value of some kind of informal training, he publicly and frequently attacked the formal, rigidly structured schools run on the lines of the French Academy. He claimed they stifled initiative, encouraged adherence to outworn rules and turned out too many students hoping for a career in Fine Art whose ambitions were bound to be dashed in a society which generally cared little for native artists.

In the early 1720s Hogarth did some engraved illustrations to literary works, but one of his first independent engravings was a satire, *The Taste of*

Hogarth's hero

(above) The work of Sir James Thornhill, the first English-born painter to be knighted, was much revered by Hogarth who saw it as a sign that English history painting was finally gaining some measure of recognition.

A satirical view

(below) Hogarth spent his entire career, from his first independent engraving shown here, ridiculing what he considered the unquestioning dismissal of English writers, playwrights and artists in favour of 'foreigners'.

The Taste of The Town/British Museum

The Town, also known as *Masquerades and Operas*. In it Hogarth ridiculed the fashionable taste for Italian operas and Italian singers to the detriment of the works of British playwrights and authors. *The Taste*, Hogarth's first satire, announced themes which were to run through the whole of his work – his patriotism, his opposition to what he considered to be mindless adulation for French and Italian art and artists, his references to actual contemporary events and people, and the overwhelmingly topical thrust of his art.

A LOVER OF THEATRE

Around this time, too, Hogarth started to produce oil paintings. Although this was a medium in which he had had no formal training, by 1728 he had gained enough mastery to paint a number of versions of John Gay's *Beggar's Opera*, which was itself in part a satire on Italian opera. Hogarth was fascinated by theatre and shows of all kinds, and in these compositions showed the action on stage. 'Subjects I considered as Writers do', he wrote; 'my picture was my stage and men and women my actors who were by means of certain actions and expressions to exhibit a dumb show.'

In about 1729 – the year he eloped with Jane, Thornhill's daughter – Hogarth started to paint group portraits or 'conversation pieces' for a largely aristocratic clientele. As an ambitious man it may have appeared that he was establishing himself as a painter of portraits in the conventional sense, the only branch of art where a native artist could expect to make a respectable income. But he

The Earl of Rosebery, Dalmeny House

Hogarth and Fielding: a literary friendship

Hogarth's art has obvious literary affinities, and it is hardly surprising that one of the artist's closest friends was the eminent writer Henry Fielding. The two men met in the 1740s, and under Hogarth's influence, Fielding turned his attention to comic satire and burlesque, achieving with words what Hogarth was doing with images. The novelist even based some of his characters on the people in Hogarth's prints. The two men shared the common aim of poking fun at human folly in general, and the bombastic excesses of the theatre in particular. Hogarth provided the frontispiece to Fielding's satire on heroic drama, *Tom Thumb*, and illustrated his translation of Molière's plays.

The Mansell Collection

Satirical writer
(above and right) Novelist, playwright and magistrate, Henry Fielding (1707-1754) was a man deeply committed to social reform. His satirical writing was often influenced by the work of his friend Hogarth. Hogarth provided the frontispiece to Fielding's Tom Thumb.

The Fotomas Index

British Museum

Hogarth's wife
(left) Although a childless couple, Hogarth and his wife Jane appeared to have a happy, stable marriage. Jane was the daughter of the history painter Sir James Thornhill, Hogarth's mentor.

The laughing audience
(above) The subscription ticket to both Southwark Fair *and* A Rake's Progress *suggested to subscribers that they, like the merry audience, would be in fits of laughter when they received the prints.*

A country retreat
(right) In 1749 when Hogarth was living in Leicester Fields, now Leicester Square, London, he bought himself a country retreat in rural Chiswick to get away from the hustle and bustle of London life. And, as he got older, he enjoyed spending most of his time there. The Chiswick house is now a museum, preserved as a memorial to the artist.

Fielding's play, *The Covent Garden Tragedy*, of 1732, was in part inspired by the *Harlot*. Hogarth's aim was for his narrative series, such as the *Harlot* and later *A Rake's Progress* and *Marriage à la Mode*, to be seen not just as popular prints, but as modern 'History' paintings, to be judged by the same criteria as the High Art of the Italian Renaissance masters. When in the autumn of 1733, Hogarth set up shop as a print seller in his own right, he hung a gilded head of Sir Anthony Van Dyck over his shop door to show he was the successor to the great foreign painters of the past. The shop was called 'The Golden Head'.

While working on his second major series, The *Rake's Progress* in 1734, Hogarth also tried his hand at religious decorative painting, executing two

Wrongful arrest
(below) A trip to France with friends in 1748 did little to endear Hogarth to 'foreigners'. While sketching the fortifications of Calais he was arrested as a spy. Angered by the incident, Hogarth painted Calais Gate *and produced a print within a short space of time. The sketching figure in the left background with a hand on his shoulder is Hogarth at the moment of arrest.*

was not temperamentally suited to the routine drudgery of 'face painting' alone and found that painting conversation pieces 'was not sufficiently paid to do everything my family required'. Hogarth had a very stable family life with his wife, although they appear to have had no children.

SUCCESSFUL ENGRAVINGS

Hogarth and his wife moved in with Sir James Thornhill in 1731, and the same year Hogarth painted the series *A Harlot's Progress*. Realizing that the sale of the paintings alone would not bring in much money he hit on the idea of engraving his works and selling them widely by subscription, already a familiar and indeed standard practice in the publication of literary works. *A Harlot's Progress* was issued the following year and was an immediate success. The subscription of the engravings, which he did himself, though he was to employ other engravers for some of his later engraved series, brought him £1200. This can be compared with the £700 which Henry Fielding got for his novel *Tom Jones* and the £1500 which Samuel Johnson got for his famous *Dictionary*. The success of Hogarth's *Harlot* can be gauged by the fact that two weeks after the publication of the prints a pamphlet appeared setting forth the story in verse which went through four editions in 17 days and

A Patron of Charities

The social awareness that Hogarth showed in his pictures also found an outlet in the work he undertook for charity. At the same time, patronage of charitable institutions often enabled the artist to obtain much needed exhibition space for British art. When Amigoni was commissioned to decorate the new wing of St Bartholomew's Hospital in 1734, Hogarth offered his services free of charge rather than see the commission go to a foreigner. As a governor of the Foundling Hospital (a charity for illegitimate children), Hogarth was also able to devise a scheme whereby artists donated paintings to the Hospital to attract the public to come and see both the children and the art, thus subtly encouraging them to contribute something towards the running costs of the charity.

The Fotomas Index

Bridgeman Art Library

Coram Foundation, London

The Foundling Hospital
(above) *Appalled at the plight of London's deserted children, Thomas Coram was granted a royal charter to open an institution for their care and education – and soon the Foundling Hospital came into being.*

Religious painter
(below) *Hogarth's mural for St Bartholomew's Hospital,* The Pool of Bethesda *shown here, proved that he was a competent painter of traditional High Art. But he was uncomfortable in this type of work.*

murals for the staircase of St Bartholomew's Hospital, the *Pool of Bethesda* and *The Good Samaritan*. These he did free of charge, partly because it was for a charitable purpose in an area of London he knew well and partly because there was a danger of the commission going to an Italian painter, Jacopo Amigoni. Hogarth had wanted to succeed in this more traditional form of High Art, but although he later painted some more religious pictures, such as an altarpiece for St Mary Redcliffe, Bristol, Hogarth was ill-at-ease in this kind of work.

PIRATE PUBLISHERS

Hogarth's profits from *The Harlot* had been curtailed by the pirating of his prints by unscrupulous publishers and printsellers. Remembering his father's experiences at the hands of these profiteers, Hogarth campaigned for an Engravers' Copyright Act which was passed through Parliament in 1735. He delayed the engravings of *The Rake* until the Act was on the Statute Book, thus ensuring that, as he wrote 'I could secure my Property to myself'. This Act was to benefit many future artists and engravers and shows how Hogarth, with his pugnacious character, was always determined to transform ideas into practical reality.

By the late 1730s Hogarth's reputation was well established, as was his attitude to the world and his art. His face stands out in *The Painter and his Pug* (p.11): tough, challenging and matter of fact. He wanted to lead thought rather than tamely to work to commission simply as a craftsman. Although constantly attacking the connoisseurs and gentlemen theorists, his battling nature led him to fight on their own ground. He published

St. Bartholomew's Hospital, London

The line of beauty
(left) Hogarth believed that the key to beauty lay in the curved or 'serpentine' line. In this illustration from his Analysis of Beauty, he demonstrates the occurrence of the 'line of beauty' in the classical figures and in the surrounding insets.

British Museum

Grand style
(right) This painting of Sigismunda, a subject from classical mythology, was Hogarth's way of showing that he could paint in the Grand Style – as well or probably better than any foreigner. The picture was not well received however.

Tate Gallery, London

his own art theory, *The Analysis of Beauty*, in 1753, which argued that beauty resided in the serpentine line. This line of Beauty and Grace had already been shown in the same self-portrait, which with its inclusion of books labelled 'Shakespeare', 'Swift' and 'Milton', amounted to a kind of artistic manifesto.

HIGH SOCIETY SATIRE

Hogarth's third major series, *Marriage à la Mode*, was completed in 1743. This satire on a marriage of convenience doomed to failure and tragedy focused on higher society than The *Harlot* and The *Rake*, though the story of human greed and fecklessness set within the teeming variety of London's people is just as moral. Hogarth employed well-known French engravers to produce the plates and gave to the compositions a greater refinement and complexity of meaning and allusion than his work of the 1730s. But the series was less successful than the earlier ones, perhaps because it attacked the very people who were likely to be subscribers and patrons.

In this same year Hogarth suffered a major setback when he decided to sell his pictures by auction to show that they were in as much demand as the imported 'Old Masters'. The result of the first sale, and of a second held six years later, was so disastrous that he tore down the gilded head of Van Dyck from above his shop door.

Hogarth's assertiveness and bitterness intensified as he grew older. In 1759 he painted a grand style subject from the classical mythology, *Sigismunda*, because he was furious that a so-called Correggio of the same subject had been sold for the large sum of £404.5s. He considered it to be the work of an inferior artist, as it was, but his own

Sigismunda was rejected by Sir Richard Grosvenor, his potential client, and Hogarth gave directions before his death that it should not be sold for less than £500. In the early 1760s a brief, late foray into political satire together with a hostile engraved portrait of John Wilkes and a public argument with Charles Churchill, both former friends, showed that his fighting spirit was with him till the end. He died in 1764, still battling to get his *Sigismunda* engraved, still hostile to the fashionable and unquestionable 'Old Masters', still attacking the picture dealers whose interest, he wrote with all the resentment toward them he had felt throughout his life, was 'to depreciate every English work, as hurtful to their trade'.

A fitting end
(below) Intended as the tailpiece to the collected volumes of his prints, The Bathos *is a pessimistic finale. But, as Hogarth pointed out himself, his work should only be regarded as one man's view of the world.*

The Fotomas Index
British Museum

'The Shakespeare of Painting'

Hogarth's perceptive portrayal of character and his bitingly satirical commentary on 18th-century life earned him comparison with Shakespeare – England's greatest student of the human comedy.

'Everything is copied from the book of nature, and scarce a character or action produced which I have not taken from my own observations and experience.' Hogarth did not write these words – they were written by Henry Fielding in his preface to *Joseph Andrewes* – but they could have been written by him and they show how close his approach to his art was to that of Fielding in his novels. The 19th-century writer and critic William Hazlitt placed Hogarth among the English comic writers, rather than painters, and claimed: 'Other pictures we see, Hogarth's we read.'

The parallel can be drawn further. Hogarth's income was based on the sale of engravings, not paintings, and on the principle of 'small sums from many', as he himself put it. He was, in *A Harlot's Progress*, *A Rake's Progress* and other series, appealing to a wide audience through published engravings in very much the same way as the writer counted on the sale of his books, through subscriptions and royalties, for his livelihood.

The narrative series are the core of Hogarth's art and represent his campaign to establish his

A Harlot's Progress (1732)
(below) The first of Hogarth's 'modern moral subjects', A Harlot's Progress charts the downfall of a country girl who falls prey to the vices of the city. The third plate shows her being apprehended by a Magistrate.

Photo: A. E. McR. Pearce

Private Collection

The Fotomas Index

British Museum

A conversation portrait
(above) Hogarth began painting conversation portraits at the end of the 1720s. The largest and most prestigious of these was The Conquest of Mexico (1732), *which records a children's production of Dryden's play of the same name performed before the younger members of the Royal family in 1732.*

Hogarth's Servants
(right) One of Hogarth's great informal portraits of the 1750s, this sympathetic study was probably painted in a single sitting, for the artist's own pleasure.

Tate Gallery, London

Coram Foundation, London

independence as an artist, as well as his challenge to the accepted forms of art. Through these 'modern moral subjects' which combined the styles and devices of High Art with the content of low-life satire, Hogarth argued that the depiction of contemporary life should be judged on the same level as the higher branches of art, whose usual content was 'History', the Bible, or classical mythology and allegory. Indeed, this had to be the basis of Hogarth's art if he was to sell his works to a wide public, for Moll Hackabout (the harlot) and Tom Rakewell (the rake) were understood and enjoyed by many people who could less easily identify with mythological figures such as Apollo and Daphne. Hogarth chose 'the book of nature' as his subject matter because he wanted to appeal to ordinary people as well as connoisseurs.

AN ORIGINAL STYLE

The new subject matter required a new form. Hogarth's raw material had all the jerky, informal, uncomposed character of everyday contemporary life, and his style reflected this. The sources of this style are to be found in the popular Italian engraved series of the 16th and 17th centuries, in the 17th-century genre works of Netherlandish painters such as Teniers, Steen and Brouwer, in the contemporary popular theatre in England, and

Captain Coram (1740)
(left) Hogarth's single figure portraits date from 1730 and grew more ambitious throughout the decade. Captain Coram is perhaps his greatest achievement, painted to rival the work of the Fench artist Van Loo.

Industry and Idleness
(below) The 12 plates of Industry and Idleness (1747) contrast the behaviour and fate of the two apprentices shown in the first plate. The series was published with the specific intention of instructing youth.

in the actual everyday life around him. 'I grew so profane', Hogarth wrote, 'as to admire nature beyond the finest pictures.' By his method of memory training and graphic shorthand – a process of linear abstraction which he developed in opposition to the traditional methods of copying taught at St Martin's Lane – he took in everything around him so that it could be used later.

Hogarth's early engravings were crude and uneven. Although he had trained as a silver engraver, the transition to engraving on copper was not an easy one. Hogarth recognized that he lacked the fineness of touch to reach the height of a profession dominated by French engravers, and taught himself etching. This, when combined with engraving, allowed him to produce a greater variety of shading and hatching, giving the design depth and solidity, light and shade, and turning it from a mere pattern into a picture. The publication of 12 large engraved illustrations to Samuel Butler's *Hudibras* in 1726 marked a new refinement of style, influenced by the French artist Coypel's illustrations to *Don Quixote* which was published the year before.

A Harlot's Progress, *A Rake's Progress* and *Marriage à la Mode* were all painted with a view to attracting subscribers for the engravings which followed. Sadly, the paintings for the first series

COMPARISONS

Moral Narratives

Painters have recorded scenes of everyday life since the earliest times, but it was the Dutch artists of the 17th century who developed the practice of using such scenes to paint a moral. Artists such as Jan Steen crowded their pictures with symbols that would have been understood as a light-hearted warning against wayward behaviour, and Hogarth drew heavily on this tradition. Later on, Victorian painters were influenced by Hogarth's morality, but their modern moral subjects often lack his humour.

Robert Braithwaite Martineau (1826-69)
The Last Day in the Old Home
(left) This work can be read, like a book. The moral tale is one of ruin through gambling – the young man drinks his last glass of champagne in his ancestral home.

Jan Steen (1626-79)
The Dissolute Household
(above) Born in Leyden, the son of a brewer, Jan Steen was one of the most prolific genre painters of the 17th century. Like many of his works, The Dissolute Household abounds with moralizing details.

have been lost, but in the other instances the paintings appear more as genre pieces – simple portrayals of manners – while the black-and-white prints convey a strong moral message.

Although he established himself primarily as an engraver, Hogarth also tried his hand at other, more traditional, genres of art. He tried portraiture, the fashionable 'conversation pieces', decorative mural painting, and religious and 'Historical' painting. But although successful in these fields, he worked at them as if to prove he could do them, and in order to give potential patrons the opportunity to commission such works from him and from other British artists should they wish to do so. His theoretical treatise, *The Analysis of Beauty* – in which he argued that beauty resided in a kind of serpentine line – was in part serious, in part mockery of what he called 'the puffers in books' and in part self-mockery.

In Hogarth's later work a more direct and moral

The March to Finchley (1746)
(left and below right) This crowded painting contrasts chaos and order in the troops sent to Finchley after Jacobite successes in September 1745. Drunkenness and promiscuity are rife, and at the centre a soldier is flanked by two pregnant women: one pleads loyalty to the King, while the other urges the Jacobite cause.

Coram Foundation

stance is evident. The engravings of *Industry and Idleness, Beer Street* and *Gin Lane* were cruder in execution than previous engravings. This may have been a reaction against the refinement of the less successful *Marriage à la Mode* series, engraved by French engravers, but may also be explained by Hogarth's wish to convey a moral. Hogarth wrote: 'The fact is that the passions may be more forcibly exprest by a strong bold stroke than by the most delicate engraving [and] as they were addrest to *hard hearts*, [I] have rather preferred leaving them *hard* to rendering them languid and feeble by fine strokes and soft engraving.'

BITING SATIRE

His last major series, *The Election*, reverted to the greater complexity of *Marriage à la Mode*. The paintings themselves are perhaps the most richly and successfully worked of all his paintings in oil, aside from some of the brilliant portraits, such as *Captain Coram* (p.19) and *The Graham Children* (p.27). *The Election* is in some ways a grand summing up of his art, painted late in his career aiming its satire at all sections of society, finding humour in everything, but humour with a cutting edge of deep disillusionment with Man's actions in a corrupt society.

TRADEMARKS

The Serpentine Line

Hogarth's line of beauty and grace – the basis of his artistic theory – can be seen in the poses of his figures, in their accessories and in the positioning of the foreground figures.

THE MAKING OF A MASTERPIECE

The Marriage Contract

In 1743 Hogarth completed a series of six paintings entitled *Marriage à la Mode*, which launched a savage attack on marriage for money. The pictures chart the stages in the marriage between Viscount Squanderfield and his wife, from the first financial wranglings between their parents to adultery and the eventual deaths of the unhappy couple. *The Marriage Contract* is the first painting in the series and shows the settlement being drawn up in the house of the groom's father, who is hoping to replenish his diminishing fortune with the bride's dowry. The bride and groom are indifferent to each other; the chained dogs symbolize their plight.

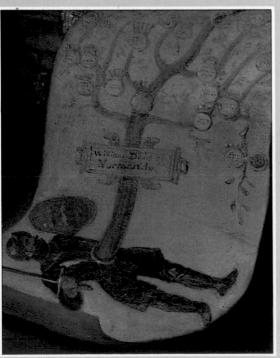

Architectural folly
(above left) Through the open window can be glimpsed the source of Lord Squander's financial problems – a half-finished building in the rather heavy, but fashionable, Palladian style that Hogarth detested and ridicules here as an example of 'false taste'.

A noble lineage
(left) The gouty Lord Squander is hoping to impress the bride's father and the lawyers with his family tree, claiming that it goes back to the Normans. The marriage is clearly to be an exchange of money for nobility.

The killing of the Earl
(right) In the fifth painting of the series the Earl finds his wife and the lawyer Silvertongue together in a brothel. A duel ensues in which the Earl is wounded, and the Countess pleads forgiveness from her dying husband as Silvertongue escapes.

The Countess's suicide
(below right) In the final episode, the Countess reads of her lover's hanging and commits suicide by taking laudanum. Her crippled child kisses her farewell while her father removes her rings.

Exchange of contracts
(below) A lawyer acting as an intermediary points to the mortgage Lord Squander has taken out to finance his extravagance, which is unpaid. The marriage contract has been drawn up, and the bride's dowry lies on the table in front of the Earl.

National Gallery, London

National Gallery, London

National Gallery, London

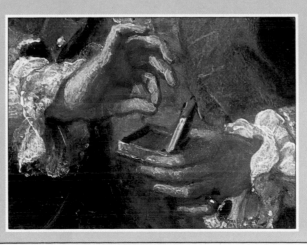

A pinch of snuff
(left) The prospective husband seems blissfully unaware of the financial transactions going on around him, and ignores his future wife. He is enjoying a pinch of snuff while admiring his own reflection in the mirror.

Gallery

Hogarth's most original contribution to art was his development of series of paintings and engravings that form a sequence pointing out some moral lesson. A Rake's Progress, Marriage à la Mode and The Election are three such series. They became enormously popular as prints, and the pair of engravings Beer Street and Gin Lane,

A Rake's Progress (3): the Tavern Scene *c.*1735
24½″ × 29½″ Sir John Soane's Museum, London

The eight paintings forming A Rake's Progress *followed up the success of* A Harlot's Progress, *and the engravings after them enjoyed a wide sale. Again the theme is the punishment of vice. Tom Rakewell wastes his inheritance in riotous living and here he is seen in a tavern surrounded by whores. One of them has stolen Tom's watch and is passing it on to an accomplice.*

which do not tell a story but nevertheless preach social lessons in a similar way, were done specifically to reach a wide audience among the lower classes.

The other field in which Hogarth excelled was portraiture. He was equally good at grand formal images such as Benjamin Hoadly, Bishop of Winchester, and more intimate portrayals such as Miss Mary Edwards. And he had unrivalled skill at painting children, as The Graham Children shows. The 'literary' element of Hogarth's works has sometimes caused his painterly qualities to be overlooked, but the vigour and freshness of his technique is on a par with his inventive genius.

A Rake's Progress (7): in the Debtor's Prison *c.1735*
24½″ × 29½″ Sir John Soane's Museum, London

In the penultimate scene of the series Tom Rakewell is in prison for debt, having gambled away all his money. His hideous one-eyed wife, whom he has married for money, bitterly abuses him, and on the right, Sarah Young, who throughout the series has remained faithful to Tom in spite of his continual callousness to her, swoons. The illegitimate child of Tom and Sarah seeks her attention in vain.

Lord Grey and Lady Mary West as Children *1740*
41½″ × 35″ Washington University Gallery of Art, St Louis

Hogarth was a superb painter of children, capable of capturing their charm without sentimentalizing them, but also showing that childhood is not always a matter of sweetness and innocence. Here the thoughtless cruelty of the three-year-old boy towards the puppy, which wriggles helplessly in his grasp, looks forward to the opening theme of Hogarth's sequence of engravings on The Four Stages of Cruelty. *The boy is dressed in what appears to be a girl's costume, but at this time young boys and girls wore the same type of clothes.*

The Graham Children 1742
63¾″ × 71¼″ Tate Gallery, London

*The father of the four children shown here was Daniel Graham,
apothecary to the Royal Hospital, Chelsea. As with the painting
opposite, there are suggestions of darker things in the work. On the
left, a clock surmounted by a figure of Cupid wielding the scythe
associated with Father Time reminds us that childhood is brief, and
the boy on the right plays happily with his music box, apparently
thinking that the caged bird is singing along with him when in fact
it is being terrified by the cat.*

Miss Mary Edwards 1742
49½″ × 39¾″ Frick Collection, New York

*Mary Edwards was a friend of Hogarth and after inheriting a fortune
was said to be the richest woman in England. This is one of several
works she commissioned from Hogarth. The richness of her dress and
the vigorous handling of the jewellery and ruffles shows Hogarth's
technique at its most splendid.*

Benjamin Hoadly, Bishop of Winchester *c.1742-43*
49½″ × 39½″ Tate Gallery, London

Like Mary Edwards (opposite) Hoadly was a friend of Hogarth. He was notorious for his love of luxury, and is shown with great pomp enrobed as Chancellor of the Garter. This is one of a series of very grand portraits Hogarth painted following the success of Captain Coram (p.19) and Hoadly makes a massively impressive figure.

Marriage à la Mode (1): the Marriage Contract c.1743
27″ × 35″ National Gallery, London

This is the first in a series of pictures following the course of an arranged marriage. Lord Squander is in debt and so is marrying his son (the fop on the left) to the daughter of a rich merchant.

Marriage à la Mode (2): Shortly after the Marriage *c.*1743
27″ × 35″ National Gallery, London

The newly-wed couple look tired and unhappy after spending the night apart (the dog sniffs at a woman's bonnet in the husband's pocket) and a steward leaves with a pile of unpaid bills.

Beer Street *1751*
14¼″ × 12″ British Museum, London

This engraving and the one opposite are a pair in which Hogarth contrasts the effects of beer drinking (seen as a healthy element in the hearty English character) with that of gin drinking (seen as the source of appalling social evils). Hogarth originally showed the blacksmith on the left throwing out a Frenchman but then changed the design.

Gin Lane *1751*
14½″ × 12″ British Museum, London

*Gin drinking was such a serious problem in Hogarth's day that an act
was passed in 1751 to curb its production. In issuing this engraving
and its companion (opposite) Hogarth announced that they were
'calculated to reform some reigning Vices peculiar to the
lower Class of People.'*

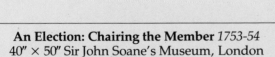

An Election: Chairing the Member *1753-54*
40″ × 50″ Sir John Soane's Museum, London

Chairing the Member *is the concluding painting in a series of four representing the General Election Campaign of 1754. The series is full of rowdy humour and illustrates the corruption that was endemic in politics at the time. Hogarth does not attack a particular political party, but rather the folly of mankind in general. The newly-elected member is already being toppled from his seat (in a literal sense) and the skull and crossbones on the gatepost in front of him is a reminder of the vanity of all earthly ambitions.*

Hogarth's London

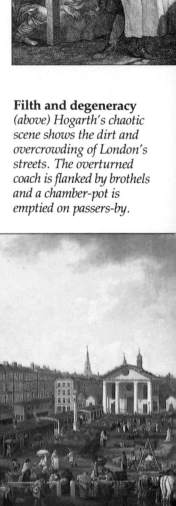

In Hogarth's time, London was a dangerous and devouring city. Men lived in conditions of squalor and misery, while fashionable society conveniently turned a blind eye.

Hogarth lived, worked and died in London and much of his best work, fashionable painting as well as popular engraving, had London as its background. Only in *Industry and Idleness* (p.19), however, did he present a picture of London as it appeared to those outside the metropolis. By tracing the progress of two contrasting Londoners, Francis Goodchild the industrious apprentice and Tom Idle the ne'er-do-well, he illustrated the dual fascination this glittering and yet frightening place exercised over the minds of people throughout the country. London was the city of opportunity where a mere apprentice might aspire to riches and honour far beyond the dreams of any village

lad, but it was also a dark and menacing place which swallowed up men and women and sucked them into degradation and despair. Going to London was like embarking on some terrible game of Russian roulette, a game in which the constraining certainties of country life, 'the short and simple annals of the poor', were replaced by unpredictable chance.

In part the dangers were physical. Everyone developed a chronic cough when they first came to London, a foreign visitor reported, because the air was polluted with coal smoke. Country cottages might be unhealthy – their floors were usually of damp mud, causing arthritis and rheumatism – but London tenements were much worse, encouraging the spread of contagious disease and endangering life and limb by their rickety condition. In London, Dr Johnson remarked, 'falling houses thunder on your head'. Work might be better paid than in the country, but it was often debilitating or disabling: London carpenters, Adam Smith observed, seldom lasted more than eight years 'in their utmost vigour' because of the effect their occupation had on their lungs.

Filth and degeneracy
(above) Hogarth's chaotic scene shows the dirt and overcrowding of London's streets. The overturned coach is flanked by brothels and a chamber-pot is emptied on passers-by.

Covent Garden
(left and right) By day, Covent Garden was the busiest market-place in London but, after dusk, it was the main resort of those in search of livelier pleasures. Here, coffee-houses like Tom King's notorious establishment (left) were often a cover for brothels, where upstairs rooms could be rented out. Publications like Henry's List of Covent Garden Ladies *were an invaluable guide to the gentlemen who visited the area, catering for all of the many and varied tastes.*

Hogarth/Detail: Four Times of Day-Morning/Upton House, Oxfordshire

London's overcrowding meant that lack of sanitation was more serious than in the country. Although Peter Kalm, a visitor from Sweden, noted that Londoners kept their night soil and sold it for manure, there were undoubtedly many whose attitude to such matters was less commercial, more casual. Hogarth's picture of a London night scene, in which a chamber pot is emptied over the head of a passer-by, was not a mere fiction. It was a stinking city, the agricultural writer Arthur Young concluded, in which men either died in destitution or lived in dirt.

AN IRRESPONSIBLE CITY

Young, like the farmers for whom he wrote, saw London as something unnatural, unwholesome, an excrescence on the country's otherwise healthy body politic. Its physical dangers and hazards, great though they were, were as nothing compared with the moral ones. 'The debauched life of its inhabitants,' he wrote, 'occasions them to be more idle than in the country. The very maxims and principles upon which life is founded in great cities are the most powerful of all enemies to common industry.' Above all, London was an irresponsible city, a place where the rich had abandoned their obligations to keep the poor under control. In the country every labouring man had a master who was responsible for him and a parish organization which regulated his life from the cradle to the grave. In London, however, there were thousands upon thousands of men, women and children who were masterless and could not effectively be tied down to any particular parish. They formed what men of substance spoke of apprehensively as 'the mob'.

There were in fact comparatively few episodes of mob rule in London during Hogarth's lifetime, though after his death conditions grew worse, culminating in the terrifying Gordon riots of June 1780. But it was certainly true that London crowds showed scant respect for rank or authority. They mocked ostentation and pretension mercilessly – dandies and others dressed in the height of fashion often found it necessary to wrap themselves in large black bags to avoid being jeered at – and they also mocked disabilities of all kinds.

The underlying trouble – the real thing that gave London life its edge of insecurity and unease – was neither physical nor moral, but organizational. Law and order in the country was the responsibility of parish constables and for the most part it was within their powers. London, on

Savage entertainment
(right) Bedlam, the Bethlem Hospital for the insane, was open to the public like a modern zoo. For two pence admission, sightseers were left unattended to watch the ravings of lunatics.

John Collet 1770. Museum of London

Hogarth/The Madhouse from the Rake's Progress/Sir John Soane Museum

London's Prisons
(left) Prisons were severely overcrowded and mismanaged. They were looked upon primarily as temporary stopping-points – before the prisoner was transported, sent for execution or managed to pay to get out.

Bawdy-houses
(right) By 1700, over 2,000 coffee-houses had sprung up as unrivalled places for the dissemination of news, political discussion and the soliciting of prostitutes.

Drunkenness
(below) In Hogarth's London, life was cheap and the omnipresence of death and disease sharpened the desire to live to the full. People indulged their animal spirits whenever possible or took refuge in the oblivion offered by drink.

the other hand, consisted of two cities – London itself to the east, Westminster to the west – each run on quite different lines. It was no accident that Hogarth's scenes of solid and secure town life were set in the City of London itself, while his harlots and rakes and idle apprentices tended to gravitate towards Drury Lane and the streets around it.

There, according to a tract published in 1749, anyone taking 'a gentle walk' would meet with men and women possessed by the Devil himself: 'Theft, Whoredom, Homicide and Blasphemy peep out of the very windows of their souls; Lying Perjury, Fraud, Impudence and Misery the only graces of their countenance. By and by a Brandy Shop is going to be demolished because the master refuses to bail some whore that's just arrested. . . A riot breaks out in another place, a bawd's goods are seized on for rent. . . A cry of murder is heard about 20 yards further, a Mother or Father being under the bastinading of a dutiful son or daughter. Pimps and pensioners to the hundred you see skulking from bawdy-house to bawdy-house incessantly.' Other and more elegant publications, such as *Henry's List of Covent Garden Ladies* and *The Man of Pleasure's Kalendar*, put the emphasis on the satisfaction of whoring rather than on the attendant disorders, but basically they told the same story. And when Boswell took 'a monstrous big whore' into a tavern in 1763 and then refused to agree to her terms, he quite expected that the result

would be a riot. However, he concluded somewhat smugly, 'I was on my guard, and got off pretty well'.

PAID INFORMERS

With no police force and with inadequate parish resources the only way to catch and convict criminals was by means of paid informers. The most notorious of these was Jonathan Wild, the real life original of Peachum in *The Beggar's Opera*. He first blackmailed other criminals, threatening to inform on them, and then when they would no longer pay, he betrayed them to the authorities and took the reward. He also bought stolen goods from thieves at cut prices and returned them to their owners for a suitable consideration. It needed changes in the law to get him caught and hanged in 1725; and for many years after that there were still gangs that picked up victims, gulled them into stealing marked goods from shopkeepers and collected the reward. Most of them got away with it, but when one gang was unmasked in 1755, the leaders were stoned to death by the crowd.

Other informers, even perfectly innocent ones, were liable to suffer a similar fate. Daniel Clark, in 1765, saw other weavers cut silk from looms and was forced to testify to it in court when they were charged, with the result that he was hounded for more than a year by the friends of the accused

before being finally thrown into a pond and stoned until his brains were beaten out. The pillory, where the crowd crucified its victims, was the most enduring symbol of the eagerness with which London's rulers handed over their responsibilities to the savagery of the streets.

Towards the middle of the century the Duke of Bedford's tenants in Bloomsbury asked him to have an alley blocked up because it was used by local thugs and they were therefore 'continually disturbed by the dismal cry of murder and other disagreeable noises'. It did not occur to them to ask him to bring the thugs to book. For the most part gentlemen and noblemen in London pursued their pleasures without thinking that they were in any way responsible for the underworld of violence and anarchy which those pleasures had called into being. This, perhaps even more than Hogarth's attacks on connoisseurs and foppish absurdities, was the true indictment of what passed for fashionable society in 18th-century London.

The Hellfire Club
(above) Fashionable society mingled freely with the less privileged in London's pleasure gardens, but there were more exclusive gatherings: the Surly Clubs, Singing Clubs, Ugly Clubs, Tall Clubs and the 'diabolical' Hellfire Club – an extreme example, which dabbled in politics and the occult.

Exciting spectacle
(below) Public executions were one of London's greatest attractions as this engraving of The Beheading of the Rebel Lords *in 1746 shows.*

A Year in the Life 1748

This was a year in which the long-awaited general peace was made between the European powers at Aix-la-Chapelle and in which Hogarth was jailed in France as an English spy. More profound and enduring in their impact, however, were the tremendous achievements of 1748 in the fields of art and science.

The peace settlement of 1748 which ended the War of the Austrian Succession allowed Hogarth to visit France, where his drawings of the fortifications at Calais landed him in prison on suspicion of being an English agent. He revenged himself in characteristic style by painting *Calais Gate*, also known as *The Roast Beef of Old England* in which the John Bullish portrayal of Frenchmen as scrawny starvelings gave splendid expression to the British prejudice that lasted well into the following century.

Finalized in October at Aix-la-Chapelle, the peace put an end to a complicated and futile conflict of major powers which had involved most European states from Spain and Sardinia in the west to the newly emergent great power of Russia in the east. The most solid gains were made by Frederick the Great of Prussia, who kept the province of Silesia which he had

British repulse at Pondicherry

(below) The inevitable clash between the rival French and British trading interests in India began in 1744. The appearance of a British fleet in the Indian Ocean led Joseph Dupleix, Governor of Pondicherry, to summon to his aid La Bourdonnais, Governor of Martinique. They succeeded in capturing Madras from the British in the same year but due to quarrels between the two Frenchmen, no further progress was made. In mid-1748 the British took the offensive, appearing with 13 ships of the line off the Coromandel coast. Their siege of Pondicherry was a dismal failure, marked by singular ineptitude, and was raised only a week before the news of the Peace of Aix-la-Chapelle reached the subcontinent. Through this Madras was ceded back to the English in return for Louisbourg in Nova Scotia, Canada.

Buried city

(right) In 79 AD a phenomenal volcanic eruption buried towns and villas in the vicinity of Vesuvius. Excavations began at Herculaneum in 1738, to be followed ten years later by the discovery of the larger city of Pompeii. The artistic treasures unearthed were to profoundly influence the development of 18th century Neo-Classical taste.

snatched from Maria Theresa in 1740 when her title to the Habsburg dominions was under threat. Although the Austrian monarch's rights under the Pragmatic Sanction were now universally recognized and her husband had been elected to the office of the Holy Roman Emperor as Francis I, Maria Theresa still hoped to revenge herself on Prussia and recover Silesia. Britain and France accepted a restoration of the status quo but the stage had been set for their struggle for mastery in North America and India.

However of greater note perhaps were the cultural and scientific events of 1748. The Swiss Leonhard Euler, at the height of his powers, published a pioneering introduction to analytical mathematics. Sociology and the study of comparative institutions were effectively founded by *L'Esprit des Lois* (The Spirit of the Laws), in which the French thinker Montesquieu made the first sustained attempt to describe the way in which societies are shaped by climate, history, religion and other factors. In Britain, the first part of David Hume's *Enquiry concerning Human Understanding* appeared. Hume, a Scot, is still regarded as Britain's greatest philosopher, and the radical scepticism of his *Enquiry* was to shock both rational and religious thinkers, since it denied the possibility of certainty.

18th CENTURY SOAP OPERA

Another Scot, Tobias Smollett, made his literary debut with the novel *Roderick Random,* a typically rude, racy work, peopled with a gallery of entertaining grotesques. The sensation of the

Temporary peace
(left) In 1748 the Peace of Aix-la-Chapelle, here depicted in a splendidly baroque allegory, brought an end to the War of the Austrian Succession. The map of Europe returned basically to that of 1740 except that Prussia kept Silesia, to Austria's fury. Other European nations were also dissatisfied with the treaty and it would not be long before hostilities were renewed.

David Hume
(right) This brilliant Scotsman published his Philosophical Essays Concerning Human Understanding *in 1748, in which he argued his theory of knowledge and meaning based on empirical lines. This standpoint led to Hume's Skepticism, by which he accepted the natural belief in causality but showed it could not be proved on a rational basis.*

National Galleries of Scotland

Mansell Collection

Stothard del.   CLARISSA.   Heath sculp.

Virtue unrewarded
(left) Samuel Richardson's Clarissa, *has a curiously similar plot to his previous novel* Pamela; or Virtue Rewarded. *However, Clarissa's lot is less fortunate. To escape an approved marriage she falls into the clutches of the scheming rake Lovelace who eventually rapes her. The unhappy girl refuses marriage and dies in a debtors' prison.*

year, however, was a million-word story by an elderly ex-printer. Samuel Richardson's *Clarissa* is probably the longest novel in English. Nevertheless the book was to be read avidly all over the civilized world. Richardson's achievement was to bring a new range of psychological perceptions to the description of human behaviour but his contemporary popularity probably owed more to another of *Clarissa's* qualities – its excellence as soap opera. Through obstacles, hesitations and changes of fortune Clarissa is pursued by the macho Lovelace. Even when the pursuit ends shockingly in rape there is a twist – for Lovelace offers marriage, a proposal that is followed by a further twist – Clarissa refuses. . . and dies.

A different kind of surprise had been recorded a few years earlier by the dilettante Horace Walpole on the Grand Tour.

'We have seen something today that I am sure you never read of, and perhaps never heard of. Have you heard of a subterranean town? A whole Roman town, with all its edifices, remaining under ground?' Walpole was referring to Herculaneum in Southern Italy – a discovery that was soon eclipsed by that of the far larger city of Pompeii. Like Herculaneum, Pompeii had been buried by mud and lava after the great eruption of Vesuvius in AD 79. In revealing so much of the Roman way of life, Roman decorative art and Roman wall paintings, the excavation of Pompeii which began in 1748 gave a tremendous new impetus to the worship of 'Antiquity', and was largely responsible for the development of the great European style that was to dominate the art of the late 18th century – Neo-Classicism.

Lauros-Giraudon

Meeting of minds
(above) Madame Geoffrin, a generous private patron of men of letters, formally instituted her salon in the rue St Honoré, giving two dinners a week. On Mondays she would invite artists and on Wednesdays writers and intellectuals who would air their views and engage in discussion. In this painting, the actor Lekain is reading Voltaire's Orphelin de la Chine in front of a bust of the exiled author.

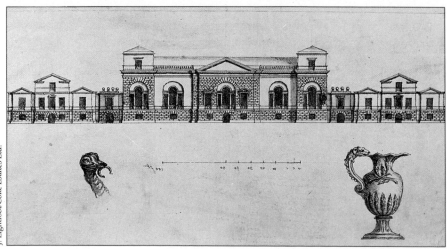

J. Lightfoot/Coke Estates Ltd.

Holkham Hall
(left) This splendid country house, generally acknowledged to be the greatest achievement of the English Palladian movement was William Kent's architectural triumph. Kent, who died in 1748, had met Lord Leicester on the Grand Tour and together with Lord Burlington, the great 18th century arbiter of taste, they set about creating a house worthy of the Earl's art collection.

Giraudon

Courbet: Self-portrait aged about 30/Musée Fabre, Montpellier

G. Courbet.

1819-1877

Gustave Courbet's paintings are among the most powerful and controversial images of the 19th century. The son of a well-to-do farmer, Courbet was born in the remote town of Ornans in eastern France, close to the Jura mountains. He moved to Paris at the age of 20, and struggled for years to gain recognition as an artist. His chance came after the 1848 revolution, when he was hailed as a leader of the new Realist school.

The Realists asserted that the contemporary world was the only fit subject for literature and art. And in 1850 Courbet shocked the Parisian public with monumental pictures of the peasants from his rural homeland. His larger-than-life personality was almost as startling as his art. But he soon gained acclaim as well as notoriety, until his involvement in the revolutionary Commune of 1871 led to his exile. He died in Switzerland, aged 58.

Rebel from the Mountains

A larger-than-life figure with the reputation of an arrogant, beer-swilling peasant, Courbet was often the centre of controversy. But his public image hid an intelligent and sensitive man.

Jean Désiré Gustave Courbet was born on 10 June 1819 in Ornans, a small town in the Jura region of eastern France. Situated on the Swiss border, this mountainous area is rich with forests and pasture lands, while Ornans itself nestles in the rocky valley of the River Loue.

Courbet's family had lived in the area for generations. His father, Régis, owned a house in Ornans and a farm and vineyards in nearby Flagey. The family's ambivalent social position, with peasant origins but a new bourgeois identity, made Courbet particularly aware of the class divisions of rural France, and was central to his personal and artistic development. He also fell heir to a deep-rooted affection for the local countryside, which was to figure so largely in his art.

Courbet's art training began at the age of 14, with lessons from 'père' Baud, a former pupil of the Neo-Classical painter Baron Gros. His parents were hoping that Gustave would study law when

The artist's father
(right) This portrait of Régis Courbet was painted while he was visiting his exiled son in 1873. Of peasant origins, he became a prosperous farmer and Mayor of Flagey, supporting Courbet during his early years.

Ornans landscape
(below) This view shows the rocky landscape near Ornans, where Courbet spent his childhood. The majestic cliffs and lush valleys appear in many pictures painted during regular visits home.

Petit Palais, Paris/Bulloz

Key Dates

Juliette Courbet
(below) The youngest of Courbet's sisters and 12 years his junior, Juliette was devoted to her brother and became his sole heir. This portrait shows her as a well-dressed young girl of 13, with all the refinement of a middle-class upbringing.

Bulloz/Petit Palais, Paris

Self-portrait with a Black Dog/Petit Palais, Paris

Courbet and his dog
(above) The first of Courbet's paintings to be exhibited at the Salon, this self-portrait shows the artist's proud, aristocratic bearing. Although it was painted in Paris, it is set in the countryside of Ornan

he moved to the nearby university town of Besançon in 1837, but he swiftly enrolled at the Academy, taking life classes under M. Flajoulot, another exponent of Classicism.

Two years later, Courbet left Besançon for Paris, which in the mid 19th century had become the European centre not only for art, but also for radicals and political activists of all kinds. A tall and strikingly handsome young man, the 20-year-old artist was supremely self-confident and gregarious, but his time in Paris started quietly enough. He began studying at the studio of a now obscure painter, M. Steuben, copied widely from the pictures in the Louvre and channelled his energies into seeking success at the Salon.

Courbet's early attempts at recognition were none too successful. Between 1841 and 1847, only three of the 25 works he submitted were passed by the selection committee. And for the first 10 years he sold almost nothing, remaining almost entirely dependent on his family sending him money.

During this period he also met Virginie Binet, about whom little is known except that she became his mistress and bore him a son in 1847.

One of the works Courbet exhibited at the Salon caught the eye of a Dutch dealer, who invited him to Holland and commissioned a portrait. In addition, he had the support of the new friends he had made in Paris. In January 1848 he wrote enthusiastically to his parents that he was very close to making a breakthrough. Influential people, he assured them, were impressed by his work and were forming a new school, with him at its head.

COURBET'S REALIST FRIENDS

The friends in question came from the circle which gathered at the Brasserie Andler (or the 'Temple of Realism' as it was soon to be nicknamed). Among them were the poet Charles Baudelaire; Pierre Proudhon, the anarchist; Jules Champfleury, the Realist author and critic; and his cousin and childhood friend Max Buchon. It was at the Brasserie that the term 'Realism' was first coined to describe not only a style of art and literature which presented life as it was, but also a philosophy committed to contemporary social issues.

The Brasserie Andler was just down the road from Courbet's studio, and he was often to be seen in the crowded café. His larger-than-life personality soon made him the centre of the animated discussions which went on there nightly. He preserved his provincial Jura accent and smoked old-fashioned pipes; he was a great eater, a great drinker and above all a great talker. But he had adopted this role of semi-literate peasant for a reason – both to distance himself from the bourgeois world of Paris and to gain acceptance in avant-garde society. It also concealed an inner loneliness. He later wrote:

Visits to the Louvre
Courbet supplemented his early art classes with frequent visits to the Louvre, where he made copies of the paintings on show, developing a particular fondness for Rembrandt and the Masters of the Spanish school. He later played down the rather conventional nature of his training, proudly claiming that he was completely self-taught.

H. Veiller, Explorer

'Behind this laughing mask of mine which you know, I conceal grief and bitterness, and a sadness which clings to my heart like a vampire. In the society in which we live, it doesn't take much to reach the void.'

In February 1848 that society was violently shaken, when rioting broke out on the streets of Paris. Louis Philippe abdicated and a provisional Republican government took control. Courbet sided with the popular insurrection, although he took little part in the fighting. In the uneasy political atmosphere, the Salon still opened, but this time without a selection committee. Courbet, who had suffered so many rejections in the past, now had ten works displayed.

OFFICIAL ACCLAIM

Although the Second Republic survived for less than four years until Louis-Napoleon's coup d'état, Courbet's name was made. His Salon entries of 1848 were greeted enthusiastically by the critics and the following year his large painting *After Dinner at Ornans* won a gold medal and was purchased by the government. The medal was particularly important, since it exempted Courbet from the selection procedure at future Salons.

The timing of this privilege was most fortuitous, as the storm of protest against the Realist movement was about to break. Probably on the advice of Champfleury, Courbet had been steadily abandoning his early Romantic subject-matter in favour of scenes of his beloved Ornans – which he visited regularly – containing portraits of his family, friends and neighbours. The most striking example of this was *Burial at Ornans* (pp.56-7) which went on show at the 1850-1 Salon.

The Temple of Realism

In the late 1840s the Brasserie Andler became a popular meeting place for many leading French intellectuals. It acquired its grandiose nickname from the group of writers and socialists who gathered there – among them Charles Baudelaire, Pierre Proudhon, Jules Champfleury and Max Buchon. Courbet spent many evenings with them in heated discussions about the role of art and literature in contemporary society – ideas which were crystallized in Champfleury's catch-phrase 'Realism'.

Bridgeman Art Library

Courbet: Portrait of Baudelaire/Musée Fabre, Montpellier

Pierre Tetrel, Explorer

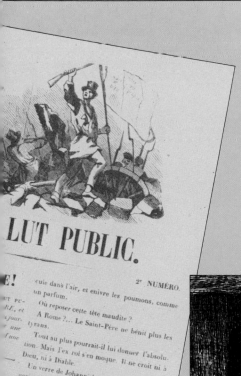

Baudelaire's revolutionary journal
The revolution of 1848 took the exponents of Realism by surprise, and only Baudelaire (far left) took an active part in the street fighting. Together with Jules Champfleury, he also produced the revolutionary magazine Le Salut Public. *Courbet provided the drawing for the frontispiece – a parody of Delacroix's painting* Liberty Leading the People.

The Brasserie Andler
(below) This etching by Courbet shows the interior of the brasserie – just two doors away from his studio.

New York Public Library

Courbet had embarked on this huge painting in the summer of 1849, with virtually everyone in the district clamouring to be included. The result was a vast, frieze-like composition, designed to catch the eye. The critics hated it. It was too big; the figures were too ugly; the beadles looked drunk; it was too individual. From now on every picture Courbet exhibited provoked a furore.

Not all the hostility which Courbet aroused can be attributed to purely artistic factors, however. In the aftermath of the Revolution, pictures of unidealized and uncompromising peasants, portrayed on a heroic scale, must have seemed deeply threatening to the new régime and its supporters. These fears were increased by friends such as Proudhon, who interpreted the works as political statements in a way that the artist had probably never intended.

A REBELLIOUS STAND

Courbet did not trouble to deny such claims. He was rarely averse to provoking those in authority and took great pleasure in the vicarious radicalism of his reputation. So in 1853, when the government offered him an olive branch, Courbet was swift to rebuff it.

This attempt at appeasement came when the Comte de Nieuwerkerke, the Director of Fine Arts, proposed to Courbet that he should produce a major painting for the forthcoming World Exhibition, provided only that he submit a sketch in advance. Courbet rejected the overture indignantly, as a breach of his intellectual liberty. Needless to say, three of his most significant contributions to the exhibition were eventually rejected. The artist was disappointed, but not

Besançon
(left) Courbet spent two years studying in Besançon before moving to Paris. In 1849 his cousin Max Buchon was imprisoned in the town for plotting an uprising, and the following year Courbet staged an exhibition of his Realist paintings in the market hall.

A rustic persona
(right) Courbet and his paintings were often lampooned in the press. This caricature sums up his public image as a loud, beer-swilling peasant – a role which allowed him to remain true to his roots and still gain acceptance in the avant-garde circles of Parisian society.

Jean-Loup Charmet

Courbet's loyal patron

The son of a wealthy financier, Alfred Bruyas devoted his life and fortune to collecting art and encouraging artists. He first met Courbet at the 1853 Salon, where he bought *The Sleeping Spinner* and *The Bathers*, and invited the artist to paint his portrait. This began their lifelong friendship: Bruyas was a generous patron and always remained loyal to the painter. Courbet first visited Bruyas at his home in Montpellier in 1854, when he painted *The Meeting*. The red-haired patron also appears as one of the artist's 'friends' in *The Painter's Studio*.

Interior of a room in Bruyas' house, Glaize/Musée Fabre, Montpellier

Claude O'Sughrue

Bridgeman Art Library

Musée Fabre, Montpellier

Portrait of Alfred Bruyas (1854)
(above) Alfred Bruyas was an eccentric, rather melancholy character, who suffered from tuberculosis. His illness made him introspective and narcissistic – he commissioned no less than 34 portraits of himself, four of which were painted by Courbet.

The Bruyas collection
(left) At his home in Montpellier, Bruyas amassed one of the most impressive art collections of the time. It was donated, in its entirety, to the Musée Fabre.

disheartened. And in 1855, in an unprecedented show of artistic independence, he staged his own one-man exhibition alongside the official displays.

The show was advertized under the banner of REALISM and contained a representative selection of Courbet's work dating back to the early 1840s. The centrepiece was his most original and ambitious canvas, *The Painter's Studio* (pp.60-61) – a monumental depiction of the artist's studio, peopled with a mixture of close friends and symbolic figures.

A BREAK WITH THE PAST

This private exhibition marked a watershed in Courbet's life, separating him from many of his most formative influences. Proudhon had been jailed and Buchon exiled for their activities during the Revolution, while Champfleury gradually dissociated himself from his friend's socialist leanings. There were upheavals in Courbet's personal life, too. His longstanding mistress, Virginie Binet, left him in the early 1850s, taking their young son with her. Courbet was surprisingly philosophical about this, writing to a

friend that his art was keeping him busy and that in any case a married man was a reactionary.

Increasing recognition outside Paris made Courbet less reliant on success at the Salon and he travelled extensively after 1855. In Frankfurt, he was treated as a celebrity, with the local Academy placing a studio at his disposal. In Trouville, on the Normandy coast, he met up with James Whistler and plied a profitable trade in seascapes and portraits of the local beauties; in Etretat he painted with the youthful Monet. He exhibited in Germany, Holland, Belgium and England, and decorations were showered on him, culminating in a gold medal from Leopold II of Belgium and the Order of St Michael from Ludwig II of Bavaria, both awarded in 1869.

Undoubtedly, part of the reason that Courbet travelled so widely during the late 1850s and 1860s was to enjoy such accolades, but it was also partly to distance himself from a government that he still believed was hostile to him. When he was finally offered the Legion of Honour in 1870, on the eve of the Franco-Prussian War, it was already too late. Courbet declined the decoration grandly, as an example of state interference in art.

Jean-Loup Charmet

Giraudon

Musée Gustave Courbet, Ornans

The gesture was remembered when the government fell, and Courbet was elected chairman of the republican Arts Commission. The following year, he narrowly missed election to the National Assembly, but was accepted as a councillor, which in turn made him a member of the Commune. Tenure of these posts implicated Courbet in the destruction of the column in the Place Vendôme, a monument to Napoleon's victories, and when the Commune failed, he was arrested and condemned to six months' imprisonment and a fine of 500 francs.

A SERIES OF MISFORTUNES

Courbet began his sentence at Sainte-Pélagie prison in September 1871. But illness cut short his stay, and he soon was removed to a clinic at Neuilly. Misfortune dogged him: his son died in 1872, and throughout the following winter Courbet was plagued with rheumatism and liver problems. Worse was to follow. In May 1873, the new government ordered him to pay for the reconstruction of the Vendôme Column. The cost of this – later confirmed at over 300,000 francs – was prohibitive, and Courbet was obliged to flee from France. He chose Switzerland, where he felt at home among the French-speaking community and the familiar Jura mountains.

The exiled artist settled at La Tour de Peilz, where he remained in touch with French dissidents and – despite heavy drinking – was able to continue painting. He never gave up hope of returning to France, but the chance of a reprieve never came. Courbet contracted dropsy and died on the last day of 1877. He was buried locally but it was not until 1919, that his remains were finally transferred to the cemetery at Ornans.

The artist in prison
(above) This self-portrait was painted in Sainte-Pélagie prison, following Courbet's implication in the destruction of the Vendôme column.

Crimes of the commune
(left) An inspection of the toppled Vendôme column includes Courbet, present in his capacity as head of the Republican Arts Commission. He can be seen, heavily bearded, ninth from the right.

Exile in Switzerland
(right) Courbet's last home was in Switzerland – just a few miles from Chillon castle on Lake Geneva – a subject he painted many times.

D.G. Farquhar, Fotobank/England Scene

The Shock of Reality

Courbet insisted that it was the artist's job to paint only the world he knew. And his uncompromising images of contemporary rural society rocked the complacent attitudes of Parisian observers.

Courbet's fame today rests on his reputation as the leader of the Realist movement. But despite the fact that he called his 1855 one-man show the 'Pavilion of Realism', it was not necessarily a label he relished. In the preface to his exhibition catalogue, he declared that the title of 'realist' had been thrust upon him. And in the remainder of his manifesto, he endeavoured to remove the misconceptions about his art and to put forward his own aims: 'to record the manners, ideas and aspects of the age as I myself saw them, to be a man as well as a painter – to create a living art.'

POPULAR PRINTS

Yet the methods that Courbet used to create his 'living art' were in some ways derived from the art of the past. In many of his most famous canvases, he made traditional use of secondary sources. For *Burial at Ornans*, for example, he incorporated elements borrowed from popular prints of the day with portraits of his family and neighbours; the model in *The Studio* was taken from a photograph, and some of his landscapes were composites, built up from separate studies.

In his work pattern, too, Courbet adhered to the conventional method: sketching during the summer and working up exhibition pieces in the studio during the winter. But in his insistence on painting only contemporary subjects, and in his presentation, Courbet's art was revolutionary.

The Hammock (1844)
Courbet painted this delightful picture during his early years in Paris. The languid pose, cool tones and graceful lines show a great debt to the Neo-Classical master Ingres. Yet the sleeping girl's Grecian profile is coarsened by a double-chin – a hint of the 'unideal' which became Courbet's trademark.

The Peasants of Flagey Returning from the Fair, Ornans (1850-55)
This is a second version of one of the 'peasant' canvases which caused a scandal at the 1850-1 Salon. Instead of presenting peasants as part of a distant rural idyll, Courbet showed them as he knew them: the central figure is his father – a peasant, but also the mayor of Flagey.

Musée des Beaux Arts, Besançon

Even the size of his canvases was the subject of much concern and comment. There was an accepted convention in Salon painting that only lofty subject matter – usually historical, Biblical or mythological scenes – was appropriate for large-scale depiction. For peasant paintings such as Courbet's, a more moderate size was expected. But Courbet rejected this convention. His huge paintings of peasants baffled, shocked and even threatened many city-dwelling observers, who searched in vain for some symbolic content.

Courbet was also criticized for his perverse liking for ugly subjects. But the 'ugliness' of his art worked on more than one level. While the fat, dimpled nude in *The Bathers* (p.52) was simply seen as physically repulsive, the discordant composition and stiff, unattractive figures of *The Peasants of Flagey* (left) were more unsettling. In this uneasy composition, Courbet evoked in the most direct manner, the uneasy social situation of the peasant-bourgeois characters in the scene.

The Kill (1867)
Courbet painted many landscapes and hunting scenes during the snowy winter of 1866-7 which he spent at Ornans. In this gruesome drama, the raised arm of the hunter and the anguished posture of the dying stag are silhouetted against the luminous whiteness of snow and sky.

Lauros-Giraudon/Bridgeman Art Library

Musée des Beaux Arts, Besançon

Still-life with Apples and Pomegranate (1871)
When Courbet was imprisoned in 1871, he could only paint still-lifes. The thickly applied paint, and earthy colours of the fruit which loom out of the shadows imbue this still-life with a sense of solid reality.

Sunset on Lake Geneva
Painted in 1874, during his exile, this quiet evening scene is one of many views of Lake Geneva which Courbet executed in his final years. On the far shore is France – forbidden territory.

Bridgeman Art Library

Oskar Reinhart Collection, Winterthur

National Gallery, London

Lauros-Giraudon

Musée Jenisch, Vevey

But in his disrespect for 'beauty', Courbet was reacting against the strictures of academic painting, where there was a tendency to idealize. In Courbet's view, it was not the business of the artist to depict historical or imaginary scenes, but to paint only what he knew – the contemporary world. As for the art of the Old Masters, that was to be learnt from, not mimicked.

It was partly for this reason that Courbet was so reticent about his own conventional training and probably why he was so reluctant to take on students of his own. When, for a very brief period in 1862, he was persuaded to run a studio, he was determined that his pupils should not be tempted by their life-classes into painting only nudes in heroic poses. Hence the spectacle which greeted one visitor of a red and white bull, wild-eyed and flicking its tail, serving as the artists' model.

This freshness of approach was evident not only in Courbet's choice of subject-matter, but also in his use of paint. Even his sternest critics did not

51

Bridgeman Art Library

Musée Fabre, Montpellier

The Bathers (1853)
(left and detail right) This meaty nude provoked a scandal at the Salon. One commentator declared that she was ugly enough to make a crocodile lose its appetite. Not only was the woman fat, she was also modern, middle-class and making an incongruously classical gesture to her plain-featured maid who responds in a similar way. In placing these less than ideal contemporary figures in classical poses, Courbet both emphasized their realism and elevated modern life to the level of so-called 'history painting'.

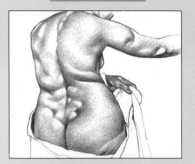

TRADEMARKS

Ugliness

Courbet was often criticized for the ugliness of his paintings – he rejected the idealized images of Neo-Classical art, and painted only real people, with ordinary, sometimes ugly, bodies. This was one of the ways in which he stressed the reality of what he painted.

dispute his technical skill and, in particular, his ability to capture the richness of material surfaces. Courbet painted rapidly and with extraordinary dexterity. And he pioneered the use of a trowel-shaped palette knife, called a *couteau anglais* (English knife), which was long and flexible, allowing a surprising delicacy of touch. He employed coarse paints, often mixed with sand to stress their materiality, and applied very thickly on to the canvas. Because of this, his pictures contrasted dramatically with the smooth, highly finished paintings usually shown at the Salon.

In his landscapes, Courbet opted for a blunt, non-picturesque approach, in defiance of the popular style, where a well-ordered collection of

Courtauld Institute

The Stonebreakers (1849)
The original painting was destroyed in 1945, but its grim message remains. The men's monotonous toil will get them nowhere, or as Courbet put it, 'in this job, you begin like the one and end like the other.'

Courbet's Realism

'I maintain . . . that painting is an essentially *concrete* art and can only consist of the representation of *real and existing things*. It is a completely physical language, the words of which consist of all visible objects; an object which is *abstract*, not visible, non-existent, is not within the realm of painting.'

natural features, each carefully linked to the next, would draw the spectator into the scene. By contrast, Courbet sought to produce a single, powerful image on the surface of the canvas. He built his forest scenes around a dense, screen-like core, which prevented the eye from penetrating inwards and forced it to linger on the surface.

This shallow picture space is also used to great effect in group portraits like the *Burial* where the figures run right across the surface of the vast canvas, with a direct visual impact that was too powerful to be ignored.

Even outside the act of painting, Courbet asserted his artistic independence by taking the revolutionary step of exhibiting his own show, under his own terms – and by his reluctance to accept the role of teacher. In an open letter to his students, he set out this philosophy, declaring that sincerity to oneself was the key to all art and that with the aid of tradition and personal inspiration, every artist had to be his own master.

COMPARISONS

Pictures of Peasants

The image of the peasant at work has been a recurring feature in painting since the Middle Ages. Indeed, in the 16th century, Bruegel earned the nickname 'Peasant Bruegel' because of his many paintings on the theme. But it was in the mid 19th century, particularly after the 1848 revolution, that the massive rural population of France became a central concern for artists. While Courbet's contemporary, Millet, presented peasants as heroic figures at one with the land, and at a safe distance from modern social issues, Courbet showed the harsh reality of the peasant's position in society, with none of Millet's reassuring, but socially unaware, sentimentality.

Scala

Musée d'Orsay, Paris

Jean-Francois Millet (1814-75)
The Gleaners (1857)
In an atmosphere of timelessness and harmony, the gleaners perform their task with almost religious devotion.

Pieter Bruegel (c 1525-69)
Peasant Dance (c.1567)
This picture of peasant revelry has a moral – the effects of excess are seen in the drunken quarrel on the far left.

Archiv für Kunst und Geschichte

Kunsthistorisches Museum, Vienna

THE MAKING OF A MASTERPIECE

The Painter's Studio

This huge painting is the most complex and enigmatic of all Courbet's works. He gave it the subtitle, 'a real allegory summing up seven years of my artistic and moral life'. And in a letter to his friend Champfleury, he wrote that the painting showed 'all the people who serve my cause, sustain me in my ideal and support my activity'.

The artist himself sits in the middle; on his right are 'friends, fellow-workers and art lovers'; on his left is 'the world of commonplace life: the masses, wretchedness, poverty, wealth, the exploiters, the exploited, those who live on death'. Yet though Courbet identified the characters (see diagram below), he left the precise meaning of his 'allegory' a mystery.

Interpretations abound: the painting has been seen as a disguised attack on the betrayers of the Republic (portrayed in the left of the picture) who use democracy as a means of consolidating Imperial power; as an esoteric representation of Freemasonry, and – of course – as a gigantic self-advertisement.

Jean-Loup Charmet

Réunion des Musées Nationaux

Courbet's Paris studio
(above) Courbet painted The Studio in Ornans, but claimed that it showed the interior of his studio on the first floor of 32 Rue Hautefeuille on Paris' Left Bank. He kept this studio until his exile in 1871; it was demolished seven years later.

An 'Assyrian' profile
The artist occupies centre stage in the vast canvas. He sits side-on to his easel – a pose he would not have adopted during painting, but one which allowed him to show off his handsome 'Assyrian' profile.

Russell Barnett

Town and country
(above) The painting shows Courbet in his Paris studio, at work on a landscape of the Loue valley near Ornans.

Photo of Courbet by Nadar, c1855

'It's pretty mysterious. Good luck to anyone who can make it out!'

Gustave Courbet

Original identification (derived from Courbet's letter) *Alternative identification* **a.** The Jew/*Achilles Fould, supporter of Louis Napoleon* **b.** The Curé *Louis Veuillot, Catholic journalist* **c.** The Republican Veteran/ *Lazare Carnot, ex-Republican turncoat* **d.** The Poacher/*Louis Napoleon, President turned Emperor* **e.** The Huntsman/*Garibaldi, fighter for Italian unity* **f.** The Farm Labourer/*Hungary's freedom fighters* **g.** The Reaper/*Poland's freedom fighters* **h.** The Old-clothes Man/*Persigny, Louis Napoleon's associate* **i.** The Strong Man/ *Turkey, France's ally in Crimean* War **j.** The Clown/*China, France's trade partner* **k.** The Undertaker's Mute/*Emile de Girardin, turncoat journalist* **l.** The Labourer's Wife/*Greece?* **m.** The Labourer/*Russian socialism* **n.** The Irishwoman and Child **o.** The Peasant Boy **p.** The Model **q.** Alphonse Promayet **r.** Alfred Bruyas **s.** Pierre-Joseph Proudhon **t.** Urbain Cuenot **u.** Max Buchon **v.** Jules Champfleury **w.** The Lovers/*Juliette Courbet and ?, Brotherly Love, basis of Freemasonry* **x.** The Art Lovers/*Mme Sabatier, society 'model' with consort* **y.** Jeanne Duval **z.** Charles Baudelaire

Berry/Fallon Design

Musée d'Orsay, Paris

Jean-Loup Charmet

A photographic source
Courbet based the nude model in his painting on a photograph – probably from the same set as this one by Julien Vallou de Villeneuve (left). In The Studio, she is waiting to take up her position as a naked bather in the landscape.

The death of journalism
On the 'death' side of the allegory, at the feet of a lay-figure (used by academic painters for copying) is a skull. It rests on a newspaper, symbolizing the 'death' of the Paris press which praised academic art, and ridiculed Courbet. It may also refer to the restriction of journalistic freedom under the Empire.

Bridgeman Art Gallery

Musée d'Orsay, Paris

Napoleon the poacher
(left) The 'poacher' has recently been identified as Napoleon III. In Courbet's opinion, he had 'bagged' the Republican Presidency in 1848 as a means to Imperial power which he assumed in 1852.

The artist's sister?
(right) The identification of the lover as Juliette Courbet might make this a symbol of brotherly love.

Gallery

Burial at Ornans was the focus of attention – and criticism – at the Paris Salon of 1850-1. One of Courbet's first Realist paintings, it treated an ordinary event on the vast scale usually confined to 'history painting'.

Its autobiographical content is typical of Courbet's work. The Meeting commemorates the artist's first visit to his

patron Alfred Bruyas, while The Winnowers shows his sisters sifting corn at the family farm. In The Painter's Studio, Courbet himself occupies the centre of a vast allegorical composition.

Young Ladies on the Banks of the Seine shows a lazy Sunday afternoon in Paris. It provoked another scandal: one of the girls is dressed only in her underwear. The Sleepers is even more risqué, but it was a private commission, and caused no public outcry.

The Trellis shows a less controversial response to the natural world, as does Cliffs at Etretat, where the large scale and fresh approach create a powerful impression of the raw grandeur of nature.

Burial at Ornans *1849-50*
124″ × 263″ Musée d'Orsay, Paris

This huge painting contains nearly 60 life-size figures, the townsfolk of Ornans, gathered together for a funeral – with male and female mourners separated according to Catholic custom.

It caused a tumult at the Salon. By painting on such a vast scale, Courbet turned an everyday incident into a historic event. It is this monumental treatment of contemporary daily life which makes this work one of Courbet's major Realist paintings.

City-dwelling observers saw it as a 'glorification of vulgarity', and were threatened by the uncomfortably life-like portrayal of a rural community: these were no homely peasants, but real individuals with a complex class structure of their own. The painting is steeped in Courbet's own experience: it shows his family, friends, local dignitaries and country people, and is set in the newly-consecrated cemetery on a hill outside his home town.

Bulloz

The Meeting or **Bonjour, Monsieur Courbet** *1854*
50¾″ × 58¾″ Musée Fabre, Montpellier

*This painting commemorates Courbet's arrival outside Montpellier in
May 1854 on the occasion of his first visit to the home of his patron
Alfred Bruyas. It depicts a specific moment, but the frozen gestures of
the characters seem to have great significance. The painting is almost
emblematic of the social relationships between the three men. His head
held high, the artist meets his patron as an equal (perhaps as a
superior), while Bruyas' servant stands by with his head bent in
deference and humility. Indeed, one critic even described it as 'Fortune
bowing to Genius'. The composition is derived from a popular print of
the Wandering Jew, the 19th-century personification of the 'outsider'
with whom Courbet liked to identify himself.*

Giraudon

The Winnowers *1855*
51½″ × 65¾″ Musée des Beaux Arts, Nantes

The major inspirations for Courbet's art were the activities and customs of the people he knew in his remote, rural homeland. In this striking image he shows the working life of the women at Ornans. The strapping robust young woman sifting grain has her back turned to the viewer, but she has been identified as Zoé Courbet, the artist's sister. The other figures in the bolting-room may be his youngest sister Juliette and his son Desiré Courbet who would have been about six years old when the picture was painted. Although the artist has paid his usual attention to the physical objects in the scene, the poses of the women were not those normally adopted for the job: they may have been derived from Japanese prints.

**The Painter's Studio:
A Real Allegory Summing up
Seven Years of my Artistic and Moral Life** *1855*
142″ × 235¾″ Musée d'Orsay, Paris

*Courbet's subtitle suggests that this painting sums up his
artistic life from 1848 and 1855 – the years between the
Revolution and the World Exhibition for which the painting
was intended. He calls it a 'real allegory' – a seeming
contradiction in terms, and one which indicates the complex
nature of Courbet's art. For though his paintings are called
'Realist', they are often symbolic in content. Courbet
described the 'allegory' in a letter to his friend Champfleury,
stating that the figures on the left were those who 'live on
death', while those on the right 'live on life'. Champfleury
is portrayed in this right-hand group, along with other
friends such as Proudhon and Baudelaire. Courbet, of course,
occupies centre stage. While the figures on the right are
recognizable portraits of Courbet's colleagues, those on
the left – whom the artist originally described as 'types' –
have only recently been given individual identifications
by the art historian Hélène Toussaint. They include a
disguised portrait of the Emperor Napoleon III and various
ex-Republican turncoats, along with European freedom
fighters, whom Napoleon and his ministers were
supporting – perhaps simply to consolidate their power.
The selection committee of the World Exhibition did
not recognize any such subversive message in the painting,
but they rejected it even so. It became the centre-piece of
Courbet's one-man show, the 'Pavilion of Realism'.*

Bulloz

Young Ladies on the Banks of the Seine *1856-7*
68½″ × 78¾″ Petit Palais, Paris

Begun in Ornans in 1856 and finished in Paris in time for the 1857 Salon, this painting of two young women resting in the shade after a Sunday walk along the river shocked polite Parisian society. While the girl in the background leans against a tree-trunk, resting her chin in her lace-mittened hand, her friend has stripped off her dress and sprawled out on the grass: she lies on the warm riverbank in her chemise, corset and petticoats. Her eyes are half-closed in a suggestive sideways gaze which implies the presence of an observer – presumably a male. Proudhon interpreted the painting as a comment on the loose morals of 'kept women', but it seems more likely that Courbet simply delighted in the lazy sensuousness of the weekend scene, and the delicate textures of the girls' fashionable clothes.

The Trellis *1863*
43¼″ × 53″ Toledo Museum of Art, Ohio

In 1862 Courbet began a year-long visit to his friend Étienne Baudry
at his château near Saintes in France. Perhaps inspired by his
friend's interest in botany, he painted a great number of flower
pictures during his stay. This is one of the most delightful examples.
Divided into two distinct sections, it shows a gorgeous display of
blooms being tended by a young woman, whose floral-print dress
echoes the flowers on the trellis. It recalls the symbolic flower paintings
of the 17th century Dutch Masters which glorified love and youth.
Grouped together on the trellis are flowers which bloom in spring,
summer and autumn – symbolizing the stages of life and love. But
Courbet's typical shallow picture space has left little room for the girl
herself; with her darkly outlined face, she appears like a cut-out.

The Sleepers 1866
53″ × 78¾″ Petit Palais, Paris

Courbet painted this sensuous picture of lesbian love for Kahlil Bey, a wealthy Turk with an extravagant taste for erotica. Whistler's mistress Jo Heffernan modelled for one of the lovers, whose lost innocence is symbolized by the broken string of pearls.

Cliffs at Etretat after the Storm 1869
52¼″ × 63¾″ Musée d'Orsay, Paris

The dramatic shoreline at Etretat in Normandy attracted painters throughout the 19th century. Courbet painted this magnificent, delicately balanced composition during the summer of 1869, but dated it '70'.

Politics of the People

Born of peasant stock, the political philosopher Pierre-Joseph Proudhon dreamed of creating a utopian workers' state. But when the revolution came, it brought a bloodbath, not an earthly paradise.

Bulloz

G. Courbet/Proudhon and his children/Petit Palais, Paris

of grammar, ancient languages and theology. His gift for learning so impressed the Academy of Besançon that in 1838 he was awarded a scholarship, which allowed him to move to Paris and undertake a regular course of study. But the fruits of this learning did not please Proudhon's sponsors. In 1840, the year Courbet himself arrived in Paris, the unruly young printer produced *What is Property?*, a sensational tract whose well-known answer 'property is theft' made him famous overnight.

The ideas put forward in this and subsequent books reflected Proudhon's peasant-craftsman background and appealed most to those radical Frenchmen who had also moved from the countryside to the growing industrial cities. Proudhon's philosophy, which is often called 'mutualism', sought an economic solution to the injustices of commercial exploitation. Dismissing the revolutionary overhaul of the state urged by other radical thinkers, Proudhon wished to dispense with the state altogether. Instead he called for 'anarchy', a harmonious society where

'In 1848', claimed Courbet long afterwards, 'there were only two men ready: me and Proudhon.' In that year the people of Paris had risen against the government of Louis Philippe, only to replace him with Louis-Napoleon, the adventurer nephew of Bonaparte himself. Implicit in Courbet's boast was a view of himself as a shrewd and committed revolutionary, whose social ideas were ahead of his time. But he in fact was no more than a spectator in those turbulent February days. It was Proudhon alone – Courbet's friend and compatriot from the Jura hills – who could really claim to have anticipated the events and sought to shape them.

A founding father of the international anarchist movement, Pierre-Joseph Proudhon had been born in 1809 in the provincial city of Besançon, just a few miles from Courbet's birthplace at Ornans. Proudhon's parents were both of peasant stock. His father was a cooper-brewer, his mother a cook, and he himself was apprenticed to a printer. This trade provided him with his education, for it was as a corrector of texts that he acquired a knowledge

Proudhon remembered
Courbet could never persuade Proudhon to sit for his portrait, so he painted this 'historical portrait' in 1865, after his friend's death. Proudhon is shown as he was in 1853, sitting on the steps of his Paris home, with two of his children playing.

The workers' lot
In the 19th century, the working and living conditions of the lower classes were often appalling. Proudhon envisaged a society in which every worker would have a free and independent life.

66

Leaving the land
(right) In Proudhon's day, three-quarters of the population of France worked on the land. But a drift to the cities (here Paris is seen in the background) was characteristic of the industrialization that all major European countries went through in the 19th century, and as the peasants became less tied to the land they were seen as a threat by the middle classes.

an all-powerful, law-enforcing government would be unnecessary.

Proudhon's perfect society was an idealized version of Besançon and its environs, a network of small communities of producers who would exchange their surplus goods for the things they could not produce themselves, aided by a system of free monetary credit. By cutting out the middleman, this 'mutualist' barter would eliminate the abuses of property. Proudhon was advocating self-help rather than state intervention: for him, big was bad, and he had no time for revolutionary theories based on parliamentary struggles or the strength of the masses.

In the early 1840s Proudhon divided his time between a job with a water-transport firm in Lyon and literary activities in Paris. In the capital, Proudhon was often found in the Brasserie Andler, where Courbet was also a regular and soon became a disciple.

THE RADICAL POLITICIAN

In 1847 Proudhon settled down in Paris more permanently in order to devote himself to his newspaper, *Le Répresentat du Peuple*. And despite his well-aired misgivings about the value of parliamentary struggles he allowed himself to be elected to the new National Assembly when the monarchy of Louis Philippe was overthrown in February 1848. Predictably, he took his seat on the far left of this Assembly and identified himself with those militant workers who were agitating for a radical reconstruction of society. But when Louis-Napoleon became President, Proudhon paid for his activities with three years in prison.

Soon after his release, Proudhon went to live in Belgium, but in 1862 he returned to Paris. He was now in his fifties, and an acknowledged leader of the French radicals, but his authority was slight. Many of his most fervent supporters had rejected

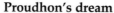

Proudhon's dream
(above) Proudhon's vision of a workers' state is seen in this imaginative view. In the foreground people are bartering goods, and on the right is the People's Bank. Proudhon's attempt to set up such a bank was one of the factors that led to his imprisonment.

LOUIS-NAPOLÉON BONAPARTE,
REPRESENTANT DU PEUPLE, PRESIDENT DE LA REPUBLIQUE FRANÇAISE.

Emperor of the French
Louis-Napoleon Bonaparte, nephew of the great Napoleon, was the central political figure during Proudhon's career. After two unsuccessful attempts at coups, he became president of France in 1848 and proclaimed himself Emperor in 1852. He was deposed in 1870, after the disasters of the Franco-Prussian War.

67

his insistence on abstention from parliamentary politics, and several Proudhonists stood for election in 1863. The master himself fulminated against such political developments, but in his last years he also found time for lengthy commentaries upon art. In 1865 he sent regrets to Courbet from his deathbed for not having completed *Du Principe de l'Art* (On the Principles of Art), which he had started as a defence of Courbet's paintings; the artist himself undertook the task of preparing it for posthumous publication. And Proudon was overjoyed to see his followers prominent in the 'First International' – the International Working-men's Association, founded the previous year.

The Association had begun as a combination of stolid British trade unionists, fiercely anti-intellectual Frenchmen, and an assortment of revolutionary veterans. It was dominated by Karl Marx, a formidable German Jew of bourgeois background, whom Proudhon had met briefly in 1844. They had even corresponded for a time. But their political differences had soon overwhelmed initial comradely etiquette, especially after Marx responded to Proudhon's *The Philosophy of Poverty* with a scathing critique entitled *The Poverty of Philosophy*.

INSTANT REVOLUTION

After Proudhon's death in 1865, the mantle of leading anarchist fell on Mikhail Bakunin, a Russian disciple and roaming revolutionary, whose power-base was among the improverished peasant watchmakers of the Swiss Jura – classic Proudhon territory. Bakunin was committed to instant revolution: the underprivileged should rise as one and annihilate capitalism in a single destructive swoop. Bakunin infuriated Marx, who believed that socialism was only possible as a development from a fully industrialized capitalist society, and whose patient strategy was based on

Lauros-Giraudon

Devambez/Barricades of 1871/Versailles

Jean-Loup Charmet

Workers on the barricades
(above) Between 18 March and 28 May 1871, Paris was thrown into chaos by an insurrection which became known as the Paris Commune. Coming in the wake of France's defeat by Prussia, this was perhaps the first organized revolt of the proletariat against the forces of capitalism. The revolutionary government that was set up called for social reforms, including a ten-hour working day and the end of night work for bakers. However, the insurgents were not well-organized militarily and the Commune was put down amid dreadful carnage. An estimated 20,000 people were killed in the streetfighting and thousands more were punished. Karl Marx wrote a book on the Commune, which became a symbol of the social revolution that the middle classes dreaded and the workers desired.

Paris ablaze
The Commune wrought destruction on property as well as life. Among the public buildings burnt were the Hôtel de Ville and the Tuileries Palace.

The growth of anarchy
The original meaning of the word 'anarchy' (the one Proudhon intended) was a society in which government was abolished as unnecessary. But the meaning of the word was soon distorted, suggesting that lawlessness meant violence and chaos rather than harmony and the anarchists became feared as bogeymen. The fatal stabbing of the French statesman Sadi Carnot at Lyons in 1894 dramatically reinforced these fears and was seen as a typical anarchist outrage.

Freedom in prison
(below) The Sainte-Pélagie jail in which Proudhon and Courbet were held as political prisoners was very liberal. Proudhon was allowed to write and Courbet to paint.

industrial workers in the big cities rather than peasant-craftsmen in small towns and villages. So when Marx found himself unable to control the First International because of the cloak-and-dagger machinations of Bakunin, he decided to write it off. In 1872, Marx transferred its headquarters to New York, allowing it to collapse by 1874.

Meanwhile, fate dealt a crushing blow to France's revolutionaries with the defeat of the Paris Commune in 1871. Courbet himself was a wholehearted Communard, just as Proudhon would have been, and dedicated his energies to this historic attempt to create an independent, workers' Paris. But the Commune drowned in blood. After atrocities on both sides, the official French government wrested the capital from the revolutionaries street by street.

A DREAM OF FREEDOM

In the traditions of socialism, however, the bravery of the Communards won them the status of heroes, and Courbet earned a reputation as a true revolutionary artist. Even Marx, usually so scathing about the anarchist dream of a rapid transformation of society, acknowledged that 'Working-man's Paris, with its Commune, will be celebrated for ever as the glorious harbinger of a new society.' In truth, the accolade belonged less to Courbet than to Pierre-Joseph Proudhon, the self-taught peasant who founded no party but whose ideas inspired a lasting dream of freedom.

A powerful rival
The German philosopher Karl Marx (1818-83, below) was the founder of the economic theory that purported to show the inevitable triumph of the working class. He met Proudhon in 1844, but their initial cordial relations soon changed to acrimonious intellectual rivalry.

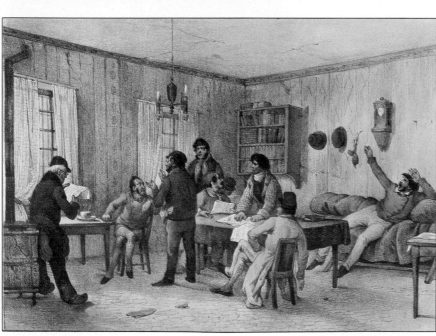

A Year in 1848
the Life

As Courbet watched the mob mount the barricades in Paris, the shock waves of revolution reverberated throughout Europe. In Germany and Italy there was a series of violent uprisings, and in England there were ugly scenes in Trafalgar Square. Meanwhile, King Louis Philippe had fled France and, more sensationally, a gigantic sea serpent had been sighted off the African coast.

Bildarchiv Preussische Kulturbesitz

The Great American Gold Rush

In February, shortly after Mexico ceded California to the United States, traces of gold were found at Sutter's Mill on the American river. By November, men were coming from all over the world to seek their fortunes and the Gold Rush had begun.

Mary Evans Picture Library

Archiv für Kunst und Geschichte

Chartists of the Common

*On 10 April 1848, more than a quarter of a million people met on Kennington Common in London to support the Chartist movement, campaigning for representation in parliament for working people.
In spite of massive support and a just cause, the movement was harshly repressed, and participants were jailed or deported.*

Everyone agreed that it was a most dramatic year. Popular writers vied with each other to find words grand enough to describe it. 'The year 1848', declared one, 'will be hereafter known as that of the great and general revolt of nations against their rulers.' A more cynical observer was heartily relieved when it was over. 'One cannot but feel glad,' he noted in his diary, 'at getting rid of a year which has been so pregnant with every sort of mischief.'

THE COMMUNIST MANIFESTO

But the real words of power for 1848 had already been written when the year began and were in the hands of a London printer. 'Workers of the world, unite!' they ran, 'You have nothing to lose but your chains. You have a world to win.' The printer's client was a German refugee called Karl Marx and his commission was *The Communist Manifesto*.

The first rumblings of revolution came from Sicily in January, but they were not taken very seriously for Sicily was a notoriously volatile and lawless region. Then on 24 February the moderate middle-class monarchy of King Louis Philippe in France fell with startling suddenness. In the early hours of the morning, during a large demonstration outside the Ministry of Foreign Affairs in Paris, a man from the crowd walked up to the officer in command of the guard and shot him dead.

This had the intended effect of making the soldiers fire on the demonstrators, several of whom were killed. Their bodies were paraded through the streets in a cart to the

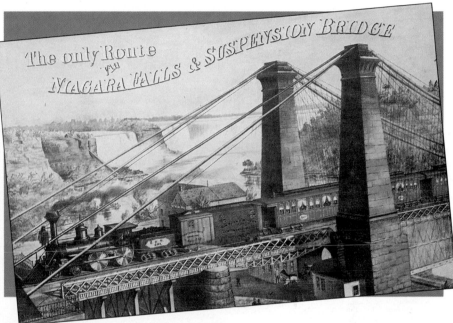

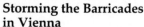

Peter Newark's Western Americana

Bildarchiv Preussische Kulturbesitz

Storming the Barricades in Vienna
1848 was a year of tumult for Austria. On 13 March, the repressive chancellor Metternich was deposed after a battle between people and military. In May, barricades were erected when the government tried to deny the reforms earlier ceded. And the year ended with the abdication of the imbecile emperor, Ferdinand I.

Niagara Falls Suspension Bridge
Completed on 14 July, the bridge spanned 800 feet across the Niagara river and weighed 650 tons. The first cord was carried across the river on the tail of a kite.

Karl Marx
February 1848 saw the publication of The Communist Manifesto, *written by Karl Marx (1818-83) in collaboration with Friedrich Engels (1820-95). It was the first charter for an exclusively working-class party and exhorted the proletariat to seize political power, and stamp out the system whereby the few became wealthy by the labour of the impoverished many. The publication was timely, and Marx's ideas were adopted by revolutionary movements all over Europe and, later, the world.*

accompaniment of revolutionary songs remembered from the 1790s. Barricades were set up, some 1,500 altogether, and by daybreak the mob was in complete control of the city centre.

Louis Philippe abdicated in favour of his grandson, a boy of 10, but the leaders of the revolution brushed aside the boy's claims and proclaimed a republic. Courbet did a drawing of a man at the barricade, to serve as a cover design for a revolutionary journal. 'Without 1848,' he said later, 'my painting would not have happened.'

The first reaction came early in March from Hungary, where nationalist leaders demanded and then obtained concessions from their Austrian rulers in Vienna. Then there was an uprising in Vienna itself, which forced the Emperor of Austria to grant a new and liberal constitution to his people. The King of

Prussia made similar concessions after an uprising in Berlin which left hundreds of demonstrators and troops dead. Revolutions followed in other German kingdoms and a national assembly for the whole of Germany was convened at Frankfurt, dedicated to sweeping away the existing petty principalities and creating a united Germany.

UPRISINGS IN ITALY

In Italy, too, a series of revolutions led to a movement for national unity. After popular uprisings had driven the Austrian occupying forces out of Milan and Venice, the King of Sardinia – later to be joined by the Grand Duke of Tuscany – embarked on a war to unify the country. The declaration of war came on 24

Giant sea-serpent
Captain M'Quhae and his crew on HMS Daedalus *returned from Africa with drawings of a gigantic sea-serpent sighted off The Cape of Good Hope. When these were published in the* Illustrated London News, *they provided a welcome diversion from endless revolutions.*

Pure river water
People drawing their water from the Thames were in danger of imbibing all kinds of unpleasant extras. Faced with an outbreak of cholera and the ever-present stench of cesspools and the river, the government passed the Public Health Act. This provided funds for proper sewage disposal and a piped water supply.

The Revolution in France
(right) The wave of popular revolutions that spread across Europe during 1848 started in Paris where people took to the streets in a show of defiance. On 24 February, King Louis Philippe abdicated and nominated his 10 year-old grandson Louis Philippe Albert as his heir. But on the same day, revolutionaires invaded the Chamber of Deputies – the invasion is shown in this engraving. The rebels swept aside the claims of the 'boy king', and proclaimed a republic.

March. It had taken just a month for the shock waves from Paris to bring down the European state system from the Baltic to the southernmost tip of Italy.

From all over Europe refugees streamed into Britain, some of them conservatives who had been toppled and others revolutionaries who had been too extreme. The first to arrive was Louis Philippe, who landed at Newhaven in the early hours of the morning on 3 March. He wore a jacket borrowed from the captain of the ship that had brought him, and he had a week's growth of beard on his face. The Queen was muffled in a large plaid cloak, with a heavy veil to hide her face.

'One Mr Stone,' the newspapers reported, 'signalized himself by recognizing the King from afar off in the boat that brought him ashore.' Mr Stone welcomed the deposed monarch, assuring him that the British would protect him from his enemies, and Louis Philippe, 'much agitated', gave him grateful thanks. The King then took refuge in coincidence, observing that he had travelled as 'Mr Smith' and that he now found the landlady of the inn at which he stayed, as well as the Rector of Newhaven, had the same reassuring name.

PROTESTS IN TRAFALGAR SQUARE

Three days later the British had their own first taste of revolutionary activity, when a certain Mr Cochrane organized a demonstration in Trafalgar Square to protest against the income tax. Since only the rich paid the tax, it was not a very popular cause; and it became even less popular when Cochrane was

The reconstruction of Cologne Cathedral
In mid August 1848 a grand festival took place in Cologne to mark the start of restoration work on the Cathedral – the largest Gothic building in Northern Europe. The Cathedral, dating from 1248, had been abandoned in 1510. The rebuilt Cathedral was to be the symbol of German unification, and a focus of nationalistic fervour.

Lola Montez – a captivating adventuress
Marie Dolores Eliza Rosanna Gilbert (1818-61), otherwise known as Lola Montez, was a wandering actress and dancer with whom King Ludwig I of Bavaria became deeply infatuated. In an attempt to confer respectability on their liaison, the king dubbed her Countess of Lansfeld, but his people still disapproved, and the king was forced to abdicate on 21 March 1848.

Josef Stieler/Lola Montez

scared off by a government ban on the meeting.

His supporters amused themselves by tearing down the fences around the column being erected to the memory of Lord Nelson. On the same day there were uglier troubles further north and cries of *'Vive la République!'* were heard.

The authorities took fright and began to enrol special constables to deal with an enormous demonstration due to take place in London in April, when hundreds of thousands of radicals would present a petition for the reform of Parliament. One of the constables was Louis-Napoleon Bonaparte, nephew of the Napoleon Bonaparte who had once sought to invade Britain. He was responsible for the area between Park Lane and Dover Street, but in the event he had little to do. The demonstration came to nothing and its petition was rejected.

In August there came news sufficiently sensational to crowd out revolutions and radicals. The officers of a ship sailing off the African coast reported the sighting of a sea serpent over 100 feet long. Scientists said they were deluded and a fierce public controversy ensued, in the course of which most of the European revolutions collapsed without a great deal of attention being paid to them.

In the autumn Louis-Napoleon slipped across to France and was elected President of the French Republic. He might have had little to do in London, but in Paris he meant to maintain law and order. Courbet read the signs and began work on his great picture *The Burial at Ornans*. Its real subject, he insisted, was the death of romantic idealism and the acceptance of reality. The heady days of 1848 were over.

Monarchy v. Republic
(left and right) 1848 marked the end of the monarchy in France, and the declaration of a Republic. A contemporary cartoon satirizes the rival claims of the Monarchy and the Republic, showing the corpulent Louis Philippe (left) and the lovely Mme La République (right) as competing street entertainers.

The Frankfurt Assembly
(left) The success of the revolution in Paris sparked off uprisings throughout Germany and within months the governments in many principalities had capitulated, promising the agitators new liberal constitutions. In May, a national assembly was duly convened at Frankfurt, dedicated to the ideal of a united Germany. By 1849 it had drawn up a new constitution, only to see its efforts scuppered by the great powers of Austria and Prussia.

Lautrec
1864-1901

Henri de Toulouse-Lautrec, perhaps the greatest graphic artist of his time, is most widely remembered for his bold, colourful posters of Parisian entertainers. The son of an eccentric aristocrat, he spent his childhood at the family chateau in south-west France, where he suffered the falls which broke both his legs and stunted his growth. By the time he moved to Paris at the age of 17, he was ill-proportioned and dwarfish.

Despite his upper-class background, Lautrec felt most at home in the night-clubs, dance-halls and brothels of Paris, where he spent his time drinking and drawing his friends and associates: his art centres entirely around the narrow life he led. He reached his peak both as a painter and poster artist in the early 1890s, before alcoholism took its toll. He died a broken, pathetic figure at the age of 36.

The Night-Club Nobleman

A cripple from childhood, Toulouse-Lautrec left his ancestral home to immerse himself in the night-life of Paris. Years of heavy drinking brought his brilliant career as a poster artist to an early, tragic end.

On 24 November 1864 a son was born to the Comte and Comtesse de Toulouse-Lautrec-Monfa. He grew up in one of the oldest families in France, with ancestors who had fought in the crusades. The French aristocracy had little political power by the late 19th century, but the Lautrec family was very wealthy and kept apartments in Paris as well as country estates around Albi, not far from Toulouse in south-west France.

However, the child's aristocratic stock did him much more harm than good. Though his parents seemed complete opposites – his father, a wild eccentric hunter of women as well as animals; his mother, quiet and devout – they were in fact first cousins. And although he at first appeared a beautiful and healthy child, young Henri had inherited a congenital weakness of the bones.

During Lautrec's early teens, two slight falls (one from a chair, one into a small ditch) caused fractures in each leg. The bones stopped growing and remained weak and feeble, while the rest of his body grew into maturity. By way of cruel compensation, nature rewarded Lautrec with the full attributes of manhood: a thick beard, rich voice and lively libido. 'I may only be a small coffee-pot', he was fond of saying later, 'but I have a big spout!'

THE LAUTREC LEGEND

In spite of the popular legend that Lautrec remained a midget, he did in fact grow to over five feet tall. It was his large head and ill-proportioned body which made him appear dwarfish. Added to this, his thick lips, bulbous nose and short-sighted eyes meant that the charming 'Little Jewel' as he had been called as a child, had grown into an ugly cripple. His self-portraits and letters indicate that this is exactly how he saw himself.

Apart from the traumatic accidents, Lautrec's early years were relatively uneventful. Much of his childhood was spent at the Château du Bosc, home of his grandfather, the so-called Black

A passion for horses
One of Lautrec's earliest works, which he painted at the age of 17, shows his father driving a coach at breakneck speed. Lautrec inherited the Count's passion for horses – and dangerous thrills.

Bulloz

Promenade en Mail Coach à Nice/Petit Palais, Paris

Albi Museum

Little Jewel
Henri Marie Raymond was the first son born to the Count and Countess de Toulouse-Lautrec-Monfa. As a child, he was so attractive and charming that he was nicknamed 'Little Jewel'.

(detail)/Albi Museum

Countess Adèle
Lautrec's mother supported him throughout his life, moving to Paris with him when he took up painting, and caring for him as an alcoholic. He painted this portrait of the Countess in 1883.

Count Alphonse
Lautrec's father was an outrageous eccentric, who enjoyed dressing up in chain-mail like his military ancestors. He devoted himself to hunting and lechery, abandoning his wife and son for long periods.

Childhood home
Lautrec was brought up at the Château du Bosc, near Albi in southwest France, among a host of cousins and friends.

Key Dates

1864 born at Albi, southwest France

1878/9 breaks both legs in two falls

1882 moves to Paris. Studies at studios of Léon Bonnat and Fernand Cormon

1884 moves to Montmartre

1887 rents private studio and shares flat with Dr Bourges

1888 paints *At the Circus Fernando*

1889 opening of Moulin Rouge night-club

1891 designs first great poster *Moulin Rouge: La Goulue* – an instant success

1892 paints *At the Moulin Rouge*

1893 health declines. Moves back into his mother's flat in Paris. Designs *Jane Avril at the Jardin de Paris*

1898 exhibits in London. Meets Prince of Wales

1899 committed to private clinic for alcoholism at Neuilly, outside Paris

1901 dies at Malromé

Prince. His cousins provided company, and the days were spent playing croquet and badminton, collecting toy horses-and-coaches (Lautrec's childhood passion), and learning Latin and English.

His father and uncle were accomplished draughtsmen, and the young Henri seems to have received some encouragement from them. By the age of 14, he was being tutored by a professional artist, René Princeteau, a deaf-mute who specialized in horses and hunting subjects.

Early in 1882, Lautrec moved to Paris with his mother. He entered the teaching studio of Léon Bonnat, a painter of portraits and historical subjects, who thought Lautrec's drawing was 'atrocious', and tried to strengthen his sense of form. When Bonnat closed his studio a few months later, Henri and the other students enrolled with a successful history painter called Fernand Cormon, who was much more positive about his talents.

By 1885, Lautrec was beginning to find his feet as a young painter in Paris. He had discovered Montmartre, a village suburb in northern Paris,

H. Roger Viollet

Lautrec's Painter-Mistress

Suzanne Valadon (1867-1938), one of Lautrec's many lovers, was an exceptional woman and a painter in her own right. She had worked as a laundress and circus acrobat before becoming an artists' model. When she took up painting, she was encouraged by Degas – a lifelong friend – and Renoir, whose mistress she once was.

Lautrec, in spite of his physical deformities, must have possessed an extraordinary attraction for Valadon, since this beautiful and strong-willed woman is said to have made a fake suicide attempt in an effort to get him to marry her. This was probably the reason for his ending their on-off relationship, which had lasted for several years.

The Moulin Rouge
From its opening in 1889, Lautrec was a regular patron of this Montmartre night-club. He exhibited his work in the foyer gallery, designed posters to advertise the performers and spent night after night drinking and sketching in the bars.

Bulloz

Musée d'Art Moderne National/©DACS 1988

Valadon's artist son
(above) Suzanne Valadon with her illegitimate son, born when she was 16. He too became a painter: Maurice Utrillo, famous for his street scenes in Montmartre. She encouraged Maurice to paint to distract him from alcohol.

The Blue Room (1923)
(left) This painting is a good example of Valadon's powerful style. Her work is highly individual, but the sleazy subject and bold forms are reminiscent of Lautrec himself.

mid-way between the fashionable boulevards and the outer industrial districts, which was rapidly becoming a centre of popular entertainment and a haven for artists. Lautrec wanted to work there, but his parents disapproved, and refused to give him the money to rent a studio. So he 'left home' and moved in with René Grenier, a gentleman-painter from Cormon's.

Grenier and his ex-model wife Lily were good companions. They took Lautrec to parties, dance-halls and cabarets, and photographs of the time show him dressing up with his friends in exotic costumes. Meanwhile, another set of friends at Cormon's studio – Emile Bernard, Vincent van Gogh and Louis Anquetin – widened his horizons artistically and helped him find his own style.

This group had been producing experimental work, influenced greatly by the strong designs and pure colour of the Japanese prints which were popular and cheap in Paris at the time. In 1888, Lautrec exhibited his work with 'Les Vingt' ('The Twenty'), a group of modernist artists based in Brussels, and the following year he showed for the first time at the Salon des Indépendants, the forum of the Paris avant-garde.

NIGHTS IN MONTMARTRE

In 1886, Lautrec's parents provided him with a big enough allowance to rent his own studio and share a flat with a medical student friend, Henri Bourges. Both flat and studio were in Montmartre, where the little artist, with his pince-nez, bowler hat and walking stick had by now become a familiar sight, particularly at night. His life settled into a regular pattern: staying up late into the night drinking cocktails and wine, talking and drawing; sleeping occasionally and working furiously.

J.L. Charmet

Lautrec particularly enjoyed cabarets. One of his haunts, Le Chat Noir, was taken over by the singer Aristide Bruant for his new club, The Mirliton, and its coarse cabaret style appealed to Lautrec who became a frequent customer. Artist and singer became close friends, and Lautrec made posters featuring Bruant with his dark corduroy worker's jacket, wide black hat, bright red scarf and scowling features.

However, Lautrec's immersion in the night-life of Paris was beginning to take its toll. He was drinking hard by now and had contracted syphilis.

Dr Bourges was there to keep his condition in check, but though the first few years of the 1890s saw the artist producing some of his most brilliant work, the seeds of self-destruction had been sown.

Lautrec had branched out in several new directions. He regularly contributed illustrations to magazines and in 1891, he was commissioned to design a poster for the Moulin Rouge, a club he had frequented since its opening night two years earlier. This was the famous *La Goulue* poster – showing the dancer in action behind the caricatured silhouette of Valentin Désossé. Lautrec was

Double portrait
At the age of 31, Lautrec posed as both artist and model for this trick photograph. The canvas on his easel displays a clever – and cruel – caricature of his own features.

immediately acclaimed as the foremost poster artist of Paris. Throughout the decade he produced many prints – for collectors' albums, menu-cards, theatre programmes and book illustrations. He took his work very seriously, and gained great professional respect from the Parisian printers. Though he would often arrive in the morning still dressed in his evening clothes, he would work right through the day without a break.

In the 1890s, Lautrec became fascinated by the theatre, and began to mix in more high-brow circles. He became friendly with the painters Pierre Bonnard and Edouard Vuillard, who contributed illustrations to a modern art magazine called *La Revue Blanche*. Lautrec also became smitten by Misia Natanson, the flamboyant wife of one of its proprietors, and depicted her in a poster that he designed for the magazine in 1895. His passion was unrequited: Lautrec never experienced a

Doctor Bourges (1891)
Lautrec's flat-mate in Montmartre was a medical doctor, who joined him on his night-club outings and treated him for venereal disease.

sexual relationship with a woman of his own class.

To satisfy his desires he visited the expensive brothels of central Paris. The prostitutes proved to be good models as well as bed-companions, since they spent much of their time half-dressed, so Lautrec maintained a studio in one of the brothels, which allowed him to observe and draw at his leisure. Many of his drawings and paintings reveal their monotonous existence – waiting for clients, making beds, eating meals, and playing cards.

TENSION IN THE FAMILY

By the time Lautrec was 30 he was going downhill fast. In 1893 Dr Bourges had married; Lautrec moved back in with his mother, and allowed his VD treatment to lapse. His drunken behaviour and the subjects he painted caused tension within the family – his uncle even set fire to some of his canvases at Albi. Lautrec's private income was reduced, forcing him to work to make a living, but his painting was at a transitional stage and he was unable to concentrate on developing a new style. It must have been obvious to all concerned that he had become an alcoholic.

Friends rallied round and tried to get Lautrec away from Paris and all its temptations. Maurice Joyant, an old school-mate, would take him to the coast for yachting weekends and they twice visited England together. In 1898, Joyant arranged a one-man show for Lautrec in Goupil's Regent Street gallery. The exhibition was a total failure, but Lautrec did not care. He had lost all interest.

In 1897, while visiting the Natansons, Lautrec had suffered hallucinations and fired a pistol at imaginary spiders. He was unable to control his

The brothels of Paris
(above) During the last ten years of his life, Lautrec frequented the Parisian 'houses' – not only for the sexual favours of the prostitutes, but because the girls proved excellent models. The artist kept a studio in one of his favourite brothels.

A new home
In 1897, Lautrec moved to the Avenue Frochot, a middle-class suburb just below Montmartre. To celebrate the move, he invited his friends to a riotous party. By now, he was drinking heavily and his health was declining at an alarming rate.

The Cult of the English

During the 1890s France went through a phase of exaggerated enthusiasm for all things English. Tea-rooms opened in the most fashionable areas of Paris, English styles in dress were imitated by dandies and society ladies, and English music-hall performers were among the star attractions at the Montmartre night-clubs. Lautrec had several English friends and an undisguised admiration for English manners and customs. The Englishman's sense of correctness and 'good form' is reflected in Lautrec's own stoicism about his physical condition – he never complained about his handicap and referred to it only in jest.

Private Collection/Bridgeman Art Library

Oscar Wilde
(left) Lautrec was in London during Oscar Wilde's sensational trial for sodomy in 1895, when he produced this famous portrait. Wilde was one of the key figures of the 'decadent' phase of English art in the 1890s.

The Prince of Wales
The boisterous lifestyle of the future Edward VII greatly endeared him to the French and encouraged the cult of the English.

Mary Evans Picture Library

drinking and in 1899, after his mother left Paris for her country estate at Malromé, he fell under the influence of a livery-stable owner, who encouraged his weakness. By now he was a pathetic sight. He would sit all day drinking in a wine-merchant's shop. One day he was found burning newspapers in the lavatory bowl.

COMMITTED FOR ALCOHOLISM

After a violent attack of delirium tremens in February 1899, Lautrec was committed by his mother to a private clinic in Neuilly, just outside Paris. The terror of being locked up for good seemed to spur him to a rapid recovery. He even started drawing again – mainly remembered circus scenes – as if to prove that he still had all his faculties. Finally, the Countess removed him from the sanitorium. Paul Viaud, an impoverished cousin, was paid to supervise him.

Viaud tried to distract Lautrec with holidays on the coast and visits to the opera, his last enthusiasm, but it was too late. At 36, he already looked like an old man, and in the summer of 1901, while taking the sea air near Bordeaux, Lautrec collapsed. His mother took him back to Malromé, where he died on 9 September 1901.

Archiv für Kunst und Geschichte/© DACS 1988

Old before his time
In this gentle portrait by Lautrec's friend Edouard Vuillard, the little artist looks stooped and old before his time – despite his colourful clothes. He had just over two years left to live.

Albi Museum

Stars of the Music-Hall

**France's greatest poster artist, Toulouse-Lautrec was fascinated by
the night-clubs and music-halls of Paris. He could capture the
essence of a performance with a few, simple lines.**

A genius for drawing lies at the heart of Toulouse-Lautrec's skill as an artist. He drew a great deal as a teenager, and this pastime was encouraged by the relative immobility imposed on him by his weak legs. Even at this age Lautrec drew with accuracy and energy, and his temperamental preference for rapid improvisation can also be seen in his early paintings. In Paris, his rigorous academic training under Léon Bonnat and Fernand Cormon disciplined his work and strengthened his sense of form, but he lost nothing of his verve. Over the years his instinctive humour led him to develop a style which lay right on the edge of caricature.

Lautrec's favourite subjects were the people he saw in the night-clubs and cafés of Montmartre. In this preference for city subjects, he followed painters like Edgar Degas and Edouard Manet,

CFL. Giraudon Paris

Lautrec and lithography
Lautrec's posters are lithographs – prints taken from drawings made on flat blocks of limestone, using the kind of press shown in this detail from a magazine cover he designed. Since each colour had to be printed from a separate stone, he employed only three or four colours in each poster, which suited the simplicity of his drawing, and gave impact to his images. Lautrec was an expert craftsman, who worked hard in the printing shop and even evolved some new techniques.

Toulouse-Lautrec Musée/Albi

Courtauld Institute Galleries, London

A new, late style
(left) The heavy use of paint in this detail from The Private Room at The Rat Mort *(1899) is typical of Lautrec's later works. The style is much coarser than before, but certain characteristics remain – notably the flowing lines of the hair and head-dress, and the way the woman's features are grotesquely distorted by the light.*

Albi Museum

Comic self-portrait
Lautrec often made rapid but effective cartoons of himself and his friends. Here, as usual, he selects the most obvious feature – his own lack of height – and exaggerates it for comic effect. Many of Lautrec's paintings and posters also verge on caricatures.

Moulin Rouge: La Goulue
(left and below) Dated 1891, Lautrec's first poster made his reputation. La Goulue – with her distinctive top-knot – flashes her frilly underwear behind the emaciated silhouette of Boneless Valentin. The customers of the club are shown merely as a jaunty row of hats. Despite its apparent spontaneity, the poster was the result of many studies, including the sketch below.

Albi Museum/Lauros-Giraudon

Albi Museum/Bridgeman Art Library

who in the 1870s had made scrupulous studies of Parisian life, of people's poses and gestures, composing pictures that gave a sense of the to-and-fro of city life. Lautrec shared these aims – his portraits are not treated in the stiff, conventional way of academic painters. He is as much interested in capturing the way people stand, and their gestures, as in portraying their faces.

THOUSANDS OF SKETCHES

Although his paintings have a great sense of immediacy, they were carefully prepared. Lautrec carried a small sketch-book with him wherever he went, and thousands of rapid drawings and jottings survive to tell us how frequently he drew what caught his eye. He developed his major images from these initial visual impressions.

In the paintings themselves Lautrec tried to sustain the spontaneity of the first idea, and he liked to work fast. To achieve this he used *peinture à l'essence*, paint thinned considerably with turpentine, a runny medium that allowed him to 'draw' with the brush. And he preferred to work on absorbent cardboard, rather than canvas, so that the paint dried more quickly and he could maintain his momentum. Lautrec never painted smooth or completely finished pictures – which he likened to billiard balls – but made vigorous images that were fresh and direct.

Yvette Guilbert Taking a Curtain Call (1894)
To create this image, Lautrec painted over a photograph of a lithograph. The singer's long black gloves and exaggerated features make her immediately recognizable.

Parisians in the Spotlight

Edouard Manet and Edgar Degas were among the first artists to take ordinary Parisians as subjects for serious paintings. Others soon followed their lead, and by the 1880s, when Lautrec arrived in Paris, city night-life was a favourite subject for the avant-garde. Like Manet and Degas, Lautrec enjoyed painting the women of Paris – especially night-club entertainers and 'ladies of easy virtue' – often beneath coloured club lighting. And all three used 'snapshot' compositions borrowed from the recently developed technique of photography.

Giraudon

Bridgeman Art Library

Edouard Manet
(1832-83) **Nana**
(left) The courtesan Nana stands semi-dressed in her boudoir, while a well-heeled admirer looks on. He is cut off by the edge of the picture – a popular 'snapshot' device.

Edgar Degas
(1834-1917)
At the Ambassadeurs
(right) Nearly 20 years before Lautrec designed posters for this club, Degas shows it transformed beneath coloured lights.

Kunsthalle/Hamburg

Musée de Beaux Arts, Lyon

Lautrec was never slapdash, however. He was a dedicated craftsman who knew much about technical matters, especially in printmaking. Even after a hard night's drinking he would arrive early at the workshop to supervise the printing of his lithographs. He also perfected a novel print-making technique called *crachis* (spitting), in which he flicked ink on to the lithographic stone with an old toothbrush to give the print a speckled effect.

THE POSTER DESIGNS

Lautrec's great posters, with their arresting images, were scrupulously prepared: full-size preliminary drawings exist for most of them. Among the most famous are those featuring the celebrated popular entertainers of the day. By the 1890s the French *café-concert* or music-hall had a well-established hierarchy of stars, and it was the job of the poster designer to promote them. Lautrec had the remarkable ability – which he exercised in paintings as well as posters – of catching the essence of a performer's act in a curt, but striking fashion.

The poster made for Aristide Bruant (p.91) is at first sight nothing more than a few lines and several flat zones of colour. But the funda-mentals of the entertainer are all there: Bruant's

characteristic black hat and red scarf, his street-wise expression, the looming shadow of the Parisian worker whose hard life formed the substance of Bruant's crude slang songs. At his best, Lautrec was a master at packing a multitude of meaning into the simplest linear framework.

Lautrec matured as an artist during the second half of the 1880s, when the Paris art world was a hot-bed of new ideas. But despite his friendships with avant-garde painters, Lautrec was never at the forefront of experiment. He shared with artists like Van Gogh and Gauguin a great interest in Japanese prints, but while these painters developed a style of thick contours and extreme simplification from this source, Lautrec was not prepared to go so far from naturalistic observation. The draughtsmanship of Degas was always his prime inspiration.

During the second half of the 1890s, the quality of Lautrec's work declined along with his health and self-control. He produced his last major poster in 1896. In the same year, tiring of the fluent rapidity of his earlier paintings, he began to use thicker paint and duller, heavier tones. But the 31 posters Lautrec made during his life were a lasting contribution to the history of graphic design. He was largely responsible for establishing the poster as an art form.

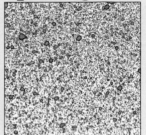

Spitting Ink

Lautrec advanced the art of print-making with a new technique called *crachis*, or 'spitting'. He obtained the unusual speckled effect in his posters by flicking printer's ink on to the lithographic stone with a toothbrush.

Le Divan Japonais (1893)
(left) This striking image is a classic example of Lautrec's lithography. using just four colours – orange, yellow, green and black – he creates an image of great vitality and savage wit. Jane Avril, the rising star, sits gracefully in the night-club audience, her lips tightly pursed, while the ageing figure of Yvette Guilbert sings on stage. She is cut off at the neck, but still recognizable by her long gloves.

Distinctive features
(right) A detail from Le Divan Japonais *isolates two distinctive features of Lautrec's poster art – his use of silhouette, seen in the flattened cut-out of Jane Avril's body, and the speckling of some areas with his 'spitting' technique, used here to add texture to the man's grey gloves.*

THE MAKING OF A MASTERPIECE

At the Moulin Rouge

Begun in 1892, this striking work (see p.95) shows a group of Lautrec's friends at the bar of the Moulin Rouge. Seated around the table are the elderly music critic Edouard Dujardin, a dancer known as La Macarona, photographer Paul Sescau, and champagne salesman and debauchee Maurice Guibert, who sits next to an unidentified redhead.

Behind this group Lautrec himself is seen walking with his tall cousin, while La Goulue adjusts her hair beneath the watchful eye of Môme Fromage. An extra strip of canvas showing a woman's face in close-up was added some time after the rest of the painting. Her startling green face, which now dominates the foreground, helps to involve the viewer in what must previously have been a restrained and balanced composition.

Cousin Gabriel

Toulou Lautre

'Really Henri, you have a genius for distortion'

Yvette Guilbert

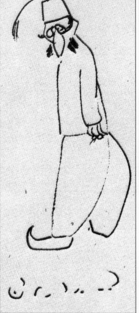

Peter Clarke

Mirror image
(above) The mirrors which line the walls make an undefined background against which the silhouetted figures stand out boldly. In this detail, the mirror reflects the image of Edouard Dujardin's trilby hat.

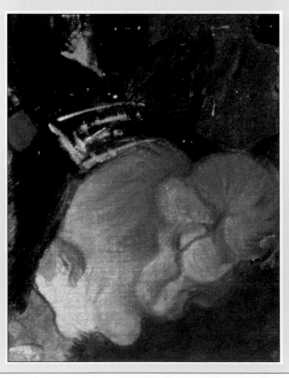

Cartooned cousin
Lautrec often emphasised the gawkiness of his tall cousin Dr Gabriel Tapié de Céleyran. In 1895, he made this amusing cartoon showing him dressed as a Turk – but still wearing his pince-nez.

Ornate head-dress
(left) This exotic hat looks striking against the bright red hair of the unidentified woman. Lautrec was fascinated by the shapes of head-dresses: everyone in the picture has a distinctive hat or hairstyle.

Caricatures in paint
(left) Lautrec often used the techniques of caricature, selecting distinctive features and exaggerating them. His own lack of height is accentuated by the tall, stooping profile of his cousin. A V-back, trim waist and top knot make La Goulue easily recognizable, while Môme Fromage is identified by a square jaw and kiss curl.

Local photographer
The man on the far side of the table in the painting is the Montmartre photographer Paul Sescau. Lautrec and he remained friends: the artist designed this humorous and slightly risqué poster for him in 1894.

Under the spotlight
A woman's face, lit in brilliant green, stands out vividly against the brown and black background. The line where the extra strip joins the original canvas is clearly visible on the left.

Gallery

Toulouse-Lautrec immortalized the night-life of Paris in the 'naughty nineties'. During the first part of the decade, he was at his peak both as poster artist and painter. Towards the end, his superb technical ability declined along with his health.

At the Circus Fernando was Lautrec's first important painting. He painted the

At the Circus Fernando *1888*
39½" × 63½" Art Institute of Chicago

An early example of Lautrec's forceful caricature and strong graphic style shows the ringmaster and a bare-back rider at a famous Montmartre circus. The ringmaster, with his exaggerated features and silhouetted suit tails, looks almost as if he has been cut out and stuck on to the flattened circus ring. The painting was hung in the Moulin Rouge from the club's opening night.

circus and his favourite clown Cha-u-kao many times, but his most constant source of inspiration was the Montmartre dance-hall The Moulin Rouge.

The poster of the dancer Jane Avril is probably the artist's best-known image. She and the other Moulin Rouge performers – particularly the lascivious La Goulue –

appear over and over again in his paintings.

Even when he was not painting the Moulin Rouge characters, Lautrec always depicted the people he knew. The poster of Aristide Bruant advertises his friend's appearance at the Ambassadeurs club. And The Salon at the Rue Des Moulins depicts the prostitutes in his favourite brothel.

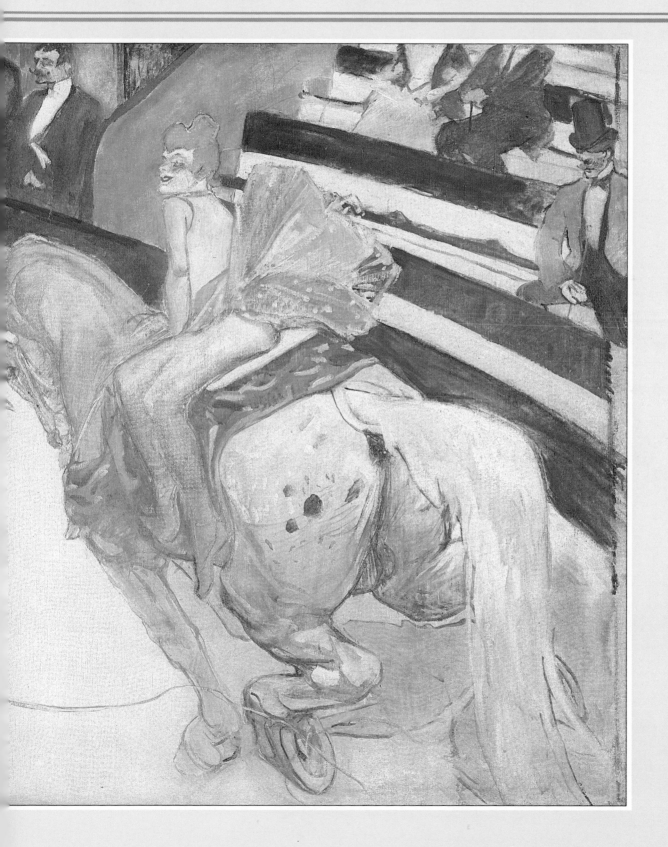

Jane Avril at the Jardin de Paris *1893*
poster: 51¼″ × 37½″

*One of Lautrec's most famous posters shows Lautrec's favourite
dancer Jane Avril doing her particular version of the 'quadrille
naturaliste' – a form of cancan – at the Jardin de Paris, the club where
she worked after the Moulin Rouge. In the bottom right corner, the
convoluted silhouette of a double-bass forms part of the 'frame'.*

Aristide Bruant at the Ambassadeurs *1892*
poster: 59″ × 39¼″

*The satirical cabaret singer Aristide Bruant, with his distinctive hat,
scarf and stick, scowls threateningly, while the silhouette of a man
leaning in the doorway evokes a sleazy club atmosphere. The manager
of the Ambassadeurs club was outraged, and refused to use the poster
until Bruant threatened to cancel his appearance.*

**The Dance at the
Moulin Rouge** *1890*
45¼″ × 59″
McIlhenny Collection,
Philadelphia

*This is one of Lautrec's earliest
paintings of his favourite night-spot.
The club's owner bought it
immediately – reportedly before the
paint was dry – and hung it behind
the bar. In the painting, resident
entertainers La Goulue and Boneless
Valentin are dancing on the bare
floor-boards amid the top-hatted
gents and dressed-up 'ladies'.
Lautrec's white-bearded father
appears in the background on the
right, while Jane Avril looks out
between the dancers.*

Oil on cardboard/Gift of Mrs David M. Levy

La Goulue at the Moulin Rouge *(1891-2)*
31¼″ × 23¼″ Collection, The Museum of Modern Art, New York

*With her dress slashed to the waist and her disdainful features
distorted by the artificial light, Louise Weber – La Goulue – makes her
entrance on the arm of her girlfriend Môme Fromage ('cheese tart')
and another woman. The front of Môme Fromage's face is cut off
violently by the edge of the picture.*

At the Moulin Rouge *1892*
48½″ × 55¼″ Art Institute of Chicago

A scene in the night-club bar is framed by the diagonal brown balustrade and a dramatically cropped close-up of a woman – her face bright green in the night-club's spotlights. Lautrec himself appears in the background, dwarfed by his tall cousin, while La Goulue and Môme Fromage stand in front of the mirror.

Archiv für Kunst und Geschichte

The Salon at the Rue Des Moulins *1894*
43¾″ × 52″ Museum of Albi

*In the foyer of a high-class brothel, a heavily decorated interior with
plush red seats, prostitutes and their madame (sitting prim and stiff
on the right) wait for customers. The artist often stayed in this brothel
and he gives his models an air of dignity, despite the hint of comedy
in the caricatures.*

Bulloz

The Female Clown, Cha-u-kao *1895*
25″ × 19¼″ Musée d'Orsay, Paris

*Cha-u-kao became one of Lautrec's favourite performers in the mid-
1890s. In this painting, she is shown removing her bright yellow ruff,
apparently alone. But in fact – as the artist cleverly indicates by the
reflection in the corner of the mirror, and the glass and plate – she is
in a supper-room with an elderly gentleman.*

The Moulin Rouge

A sensation from its opening night, the Moulin Rouge was
Montmartre's most spectacular night-club. Its frenzied atmosphere
of drinking and dancing attracted patrons from all over the world.

Of all the famous night-clubs seen in Toulouse-Lautrec's paintings, the Bal du Moulin Rouge most perfectly symbolizes the heady mix of glamour and seaminess of night-time Montmartre. A night-club on the grand scale, the place attracted people from all walks of life, who found its debauched atmosphere irresistible. Toulouse-Lautrec was a regular patron from the opening night and found the intense, vulgar scene – and the magnetically wicked female dancers – ideal material for his art.

THE MOULIN ROUGE

The Bal du Moulin Rouge opened in 1889 on the Boulevard de Clichy, taking the place of a cheap dance hall called the Reine Blanche. From 1891, the entrance foyer became a picture gallery where throngs of patrons drank and mingled with pimps, prostitutes, dancing girls and undercover police officers. The interior comprised a huge dancing area surrounded by galleries, a vast bar and a stage on which a bizarre variety of entertainers appeared each night, including clowns, singers, exotic dancers, acrobats and some lively cancan troupes.

The Moulin Rouge also included an extensive covered promenade enclosing a garden with small tables and chairs where patrons could sit and drink. Dominating the centre of the garden was a gigantic elephant made out of cardboard, large enough to contain a whole orchestra. Around it monkeys were kept tethered on chains to entertain the customers. People could also go for donkey-rides around the garden – if they had not drunk too much of 'the green fairy', or absinthe, the aniseed drink most popular in the bars of Montmartre.

The red windmill on the roof, a beacon for those seeking the pleasures of the flesh, was a wooden model recalling the days not so long before when Montmartre was a leafy hill village, dotted with genuine windmills of much larger proportions. Charles Zidler, who opened the Moulin Rouge, went all out to provide entertainment on a scale

Inspecting the girls
The Moulin Rouge was Europe's biggest flesh market, attracting male clientele from all over the world. Many of its 'dancers' were little more than prostitutes.

lavish enough to draw clientèle away from the main competition, which consisted of the Élysée-Montmartre dance hall and the Casino de Paris in the rue Clichy.

Setting the tone for the evening would be a circus-like din of music by Offenbach and Olivier Metra, played at full volume on trombones, cymbals and drums. By the turn of the century came dance fads such as the mattchiche and the cakewalk and the bands would work the crowd up into such a drunken frenzy that foreign visitors were left aghast. One broadminded magazine reporter from England wrote, 'In this place no passions need be curbed. There is shouting and horseplay; women are carried around the hall on the shoulders of men; there is a fierce increasing cry for drink.'

But the main attractions for the male clientèle of the Moulin Rouge – who came from places all over the world, from Russia, England, Rumania and

The Moulin Rouge

(left) Named after its 'red mill' which was lit up at night, the Moulin Rouge opened on the Boulevard Clichy in Montmartre in 1889. Its vast dance-floor and exotic entertainment attracted Parisians of all classes.

Carnavalet/Bulloz

High jinks

(above) Patrons and performers took the floor together, dancing in the energetic style made popular by the stars of the Moulin Rouge such as La Goulue and Valentin Désossée – the boneless wonder.

A cardboard elephant

At the back of the club a vast cardboard elephant dominated the garden, where patrons could take donkey rides. The elephant could hold a whole orchestra.

H. Roger Viollet

South America – were the women with their saucy, promiscuous reputation. The sex trade was flourishing in the fringes of Paris. Vice was not only big business in night-clubs and brothels: establishments abroad also sought Parisian girls for prostitution. The Moulin Rouge, which was considered the biggest flesh market in Europe, was glittery and frivolous on the surface, but women working in the blurred vocation of dancer-prostitute could easily find themselves kidnapped by suppliers of the white slave trade.

UPPER-CLASS PLEASURES

Although a poster described the Moulin Rouge as 'le rendez-vous du High Life', most society figures would have found the crude conversation and the constant vulgarity too much for their taste.

But a good number of apparently respectable bourgeois Parisians found the flirtatious bar girls and the generally risqué atmosphere of the Moulin

The dancer, Yvette Guilbert

(right) The most successful of all the performers at the Moulin Rouge, black-gloved Yvette Guilbert sang risqué contemporary songs in a rasping voice.

Edimedia

99

Théophile Steinlen/Bruant dans la Rue

The singer, Aristide Bruant
(left) A leading singer-songwriter on the café-concert circuit, Bruant sang about the poor people of Paris in a bitter and mocking way. In between songs he insulted the fashionable audiences who flocked to hear him.

Troupers at the music-hall
The Moulin Rouge had a high turnover of performers – especially young girls. Some were lucky enough to win fame, but most had only a short career before disappearing into obscurity.

Rouge far more fascinating than the tamer ballrooms of the Champs-Élysées. These pleasure-seekers from the upper classes would be prime targets for expensive, lavishly-dressed prostitutes who were skilled in the art of persuading men to buy them expensive drinks – and were always on the look-out for a wealthy 'sugar-daddy'.

Among the entertainers who performed at the Moulin Rouge, a few individuals established special notoriety for their outrageous styles. To promote them, Zidler asked Toulouse-Lautrec, who was visiting several times a week and whose paintings were on display in the foyer, to prepare the poster for the 1891 season.

LA GOULUE

Toulouse-Lautrec chose as his subject a 20-year-old dancer called 'La Goulue' (the insatiable) who had been lured away from the Elysée-Montmartre. Her cancan act was a sensation. She was a plump, pale woman, tightly bound in a black dress which featured a tumbling froth of skirts, swirling lace and fancy undergarments trimmed with attractive coloured ribbons.

Over the years the cancan style had achieved a reputation as a kind of mildly erotic ritual in which

Dancing the cancan
Each evening the performance opened with the cancan, to the music of Offenbach played at full volume. The dancers wore black stockings and frothy undergarments, their virtuoso display always ending with the splits.

and always had the crowds gathering round in amazement. Another dancer, Jane Avril, also demonstrated a frenetic, nervous energy, but her style was contrastingly sophisticated and refined. Her English chorus-girl costume was restrained compared to the tawdry excesses of some of the dancers and she went on to enjoy a successful solo career. Like La Goulue, however, she too died in poverty in the 1940s. Yvette Guilbert, the singer with the long black gloves, was one of the few artistes to develop her career successfully. She left the Moulin Rouge to become an international star, touring Britain and the United States.

CHA-U-KAO THE FEMALE CLOWN

After La Goulue's departure from the scene, a large female clown-cum-dancer won favour with the crowds. Dressed in Japanese costume and boasting the pseudo-Japanese name of Cha-U-Kao, she rode horses bareback to sustain the magic of the Moulin Rouge for a few more years. Japanese culture was very fashionable in the 1890s, and Toulouse-Lautrec himself enjoyed dressing up for his friends as either a samurai warrior or a geisha girl.

But the tearaway life of hard-drinking and constant performing inevitably took its toll on most of the overnight celebrities of the Moulin Rouge. Toulouse-Lautrec had to move fast sketching faces and figures when the light permitted, before his glittering subjects were abandoned to obscurity by alcohol, or a fickle change in fashion.

the beauty of the dancer mattered less than the skill of the performance – which always ended with the splits.

La Goulue's troupe – who all had cheeky underworld names such as 'Grille d'Egout' (sewer trap); 'La Môme Fromage' (cheese tart) and 'Nini Patte en l'Air' (Nini leg-in-air) – specialized in a very popular routine called the 'quadrille naturaliste' which involved much high raising of legs in the air.

La Goulue's reign as the queen of the Montmartre showgirls was characteristically short. After five years, having grown too fat, she was forced to make her living by exhibiting herself in a fairground booth, then went on to work as an animal trainer. Finally she became a brothel servant and even sold sweets for a time outside the Moulin Rouge. In 1929 she died an alcoholic derelict.

THE BONELESS WONDER

One of La Goulue's male dancing partners at the Moulin Rouge was Valentin, the owner of a small Montmartre café. His extraordinary contortions on the dance floor earned him the nickname 'Le Désossé' – the boneless wonder. A short, curiously double-jointed figure, his frenetic movements made it seem as if his body was made of rubber,

La Goulue's sad end
(right) For five years the star dancer at the Moulin Rouge, La Goulue finally grew too fat, and was forced to perform in a fairground booth. The photograph shows her on the steps of her caravan.

H. Roger Viollet

While Toulouse-Lautrec was painting in the night-clubs of Paris, France's Republican government was struggling to assert its power. Failure to quell terrorism left it looking foolish, and in June the president himself was stabbed by an Italian anarchist. So the press howled with triumph when Captain Dreyfus was convicted of spying – yet this would prove the government's worst mistake.

The Mansell Collection

The Dreyfus affair
(left) On 15 October 1894, the Jewish army officer Alfred Dreyfus was accused of selling secrets to Germany. As a result of forged evidence he was found guilty, stripped of his rank and sent to Devil's Island. Twelve years later, after a great political upheaval, Dreyfus was declared innocent, and awarded the Legion of Honour.

The last Tsar of Russia
(right) Nicholas II succeeded his father in 1894 and was crowned in Moscow the next year. He was an autocratic monarch who distrusted his ministers, and when his court fell under the spell of the evil Rasputin the Tsar lost all support. In 1917, at the start of the Russian Revolution, he was forced to abdicate and was murdered a year later.

Tower Bridge opens
Tower Bridge was opened by the Prince of Wales on 30 June. It was designed by the same architect as Smithfield and Billingsgate markets – Sir Horace Jones – and engineer Sir John Wolfe Barry. The two halves of the 250-foot centre span were originally operated by steam power.

The Guildhall Gallery

W.L. Wyllie/The Opening of Tower Bridge

On New Year's Day, police throughout France made surprise raids on anarchist cells. In Paris, Lyon, Rouen, Lille and many other towns, leaders of the terrorist organizations were arrested and taken to prison while their homes were systematically searched. Somehow the anarchists had been forewarned: not a single document of importance, not one piece of evidence which might incriminate them was found.

INVENTING THE EVIDENCE

The French government, under attack for its weakness in the face of terrorism, had hoped to demonstrate its firmness. Instead it had been made to look extremely foolish. In official quarters the lesson was well learned. Next time there must be no failure: charges must be made to stick, evidence must be found. If it was not, then it must be manufactured. The learning of this lesson would have shattering effects before the year was out, in the case of Alfred Dreyfus.

A few days later came an odd snippet of news from Russia. The official prayers cursing the French – said regularly ever since Napoleon's invasion of 1812 – had been dropped. What could this mean? Tsar Alexander III was generally regarded as the most autocratic of European rulers. Terrible stories were leaking out of the Tsar's prisons of merciless beatings, of limbs lopped off with sabres, of prisoners brought by famine to open cannibalism. It was unthinkable that Republican France, the champion of liberalism and progress, should be moving closer to this reactionary tyrant.

J-L Charmet

Mary Evans Picture Library

Aubrey Beardsley's Yellow Book
(above) The illustrator of Oscar Wilde's Salome, *Beardsley (1872-98) achieved fame at an early age. Much of his work was satirical, and some of it bordered on the obscene. In 1894 he began illustrating the controversial literary magazine* The Yellow Book. *Beardsley was just 26 when he died.*

Nevertheless she was. On 4 January 1894 the government gave its approval to a secret military alliance with the Russians. Meanwhile financiers in Paris were making huge profits out of loans to Russia and the money was being used to extend the Trans-Siberian railway. At the end of that particular line lay China and Japan – rich prizes for Russian autocracy and French capitalism alike. The Russians had successfully weaned the French from their alliance with Britain.

DECADENT PARIS

For their part the British saw the French not as capitalist imperialists but as revolutionary republicans who were little better than the terrorists they were trying to suppress. In February, when an anarchist was blown up by his own bomb, near Greenwich Observatory, the British newspapers made much of the fact that he was French. Paris, above all, was seen as the home of subversion and immorality. 'What mischief that very attractive Paris has done to English society, to the stage and to literature,' wrote the Princess Royal to Queen Victoria, *'What harm* to the young and brilliant aristocracy of London!'

And the shady world which Toulouse-Lautrec inhabited and depicted, the world of cabarets and brothels and absinthe, was the quintessence of Parisian depravity. Needless to say, when Lautrec came to London in 1894, he mixed not with respectable society, but with extremely suspect writers and artists who were openly promoting paganism in the pages of the newly founded *Yellow Book.*

Mary Evans Picture Library

Lauros-Giraudon

Assassination of a president
(left) Sadi Carnot, the fourth president of France's Third Republic, was murdered by an Italian anarchist in 1894 at the height of his popularity. He had a reputation for integrity.

The first movies
(above) In 1894 the French Lumière brothers produced the cinematograph – a projector for moving pictures. That same year, a 'kinetoscope' parlour opened in New York, using Thomas Edison's peephole machine.

Spectrum Colour Library

The irony was that most Frenchmen found Paris equally repugnant. France was a country of farmers and small traders, deeply conservative, traditionally religious and very suspicious of the corruption and violence which marked political life in Paris. But the anarchist outrages continued unchecked and in June, the President of the Republic was stabbed to death by an Italian terrorist. His successor came under immediate and vicious attack in the radical press.

THE PRESS'S OWN SCANDAL

But towards the end of the year, the press found itself smeared with its own scandal-mongering. It was revealed that a group of newspaper barons had formed 'a syndicate for turning to profitable account all sorts of scandals – social, financial or judicial – of which the heroes might desire to purchase the silence of the newspapers'. A most unedifying situation followed in which cynicism and chicanery came to the fore. As prominent journalists and proprietors were arrested on blackmail and corruption charges, the disgust which provincial Frenchmen felt for their capital deepened still further.

One of the few institutions which had so far escaped the rising tide of discredit and disillusionment was the French army. France's proud military tradition, with its echoes both of revolutionary fervour and of imperial conquest, perhaps could still re-unite a divided and embittered country. But even in the army all was not well: it was known that secrets were being passed to the Germans, but nobody could find the spy.

The Olympic Games
Baron Pierre de Coubertin, a French scholar and educator, was the driving force behind the revival of the Olympic Games. In 1894 he organized an international conference in Paris at which delegates from 12 countries voted to hold the first modern Games in Athens in 1896.

Mary Evans Picture Library

Blackpool Tower
The brain-child of a London businessman who had been impressed by the Eiffel Tower, Blackpool's famous landmark took three years to build and the opening ceremony took place in spring 1894. It is 520 feet high and houses a circus and a ballroom. The present cabaret lounge was originally a zoo.

Svengali the hypnotist
In Trilby, *the famous novel by George du Maurier published in 1894, Trilby is an artist's model in Paris with whom various English students fall in love. Hypnotised by Svengali, she becomes a singer – but loses her voice when he dies.*

" 'ET MAINTENANT DORS, MA MIGNONNE !' "

The Mansell Collection

105

Mercier, the War Minister, was under constant attack in the Chamber of Deputies and the press was at his heels. Finally, at the end of October, the anti-Jewish paper *La Libre Parole* revealed that a Jewish officer, Captain Dreyfus, had been charged with treason.

DREYFUS FRAMED

He was the perfect scapegoat, a hated Jew on whose shoulders the guilt of a whole nation could be loaded. 'If Dreyfus is acquitted, Mercier goes!' screamed the press. It was not only Mercier, but the good name of the army, the credibility of the Republic, and the honour of France that depended on Dreyfus being convicted. As a direct consequence, the lesson of January

was applied with rigorous and ruthless efficiency.

The only evidence against Dreyfus was a letter that the handwriting experts swore he could not have written. Their opinion was set aside and documents were falsified in order to make a case against him. He was found guilty at a secret court martial and condemned to degradation and deportation for life and was sent to the penal colony on Devil's Island, Guiana. Although he protested his innocence, press and public were delighted and the honour of the army was saved. The only complaint, even among those who were later to support his cause, was that he had not been condemned to death. But the price had been higher than anyone realized. The controversy over Dreyfus and his eventual rehabilitation was destined to tear apart the whole fabric of French society.

Mary Evans Picture Library

Felix Greene/Camerapix Hutchison

An explorer in Tibet
The Swede Sven Hedin, one of the greatest explorers of his age, was the first person to produce a detailed map of Tibet. In 1894 he was in Tibet during a five-year expedition in which he crossed a vast area of Asia from the Urals to Peking, making several important geographical and archaeological discoveries.

Sarah Bernhardt
In 1894 the famous French actress (1844-1923) visited London to perform at Daly's Theatre. Her London debut in 1879 had been a huge success and inspired a series of world tours. Later in life 'the divine Sarah' had a leg amputated, but this did not prevent her from either acting or touring.

Montagu Motor Museum

The Paris-Rouen race
This race, held on 22 July, was the first of the great motor rallies. Twenty-one vehicles started, and a Peugeot was awarded the first prize of 5000 francs. The competitors had an hour's pause for lunch.

DIEGO RIVERA

1886-1957

Diego Rivera was one of the most colourful and charismatic figures of 20th-century art. Born in Mexico and trained as an academic painter, Rivera travelled to Europe and became a leading Cubist and member of the bohemian Parisian art world. When he returned to Mexico in 1921, at the end of its long and bloody Revolution, he became involved in the radical cause and joined the Mexican Communist Party.

Rivera's work then took on a different, more public complexion in a series of monumentally realist murals in government buildings. These frescoes, which depicted the Indian past and the mechanized future of the American continent, created an idealized and popular vision of the gains of the Mexican Revolution. They proved enormously influential in Mexico and the United States during the 1920s and 1930s.

The Mexican Giant

Diego Rivera was a larger-than-life character whose monumental mural schemes were inspired by his tremendous enthusiasm for the revolutionary cause.

Key Dates

1886 born in Guanajuato, Mexico

1898-1907 studies in Mexico City, then Madrid

1909 lives in Paris

1921 returns to Mexico; starts work on his first murals

1922 marries Guadalupe

1923-27 works on murals at the Ministry of Education, Mexico City

1927-1928 works in Moscow

1929 marries Frida Kahlo

1930-34 works in USA

1938-1939 close association with Trotsky and André Breton; makes Surrealist paintings.

1954 Frida dies

1957 Rivera dies in Mexico City

'Diego greeted me at the Railway Station . . . I had heard earlier that he was one of the founders of the Communist Party in Mexico, that he was greatest Mexican painter, and that he could hit a coin thrown in the air with his revolver . . . he turned out to be a formidable man with quite a paunch and with a broad ever-smiling face . . .' Such was the Russian revolutionary poet Vladimir Mayakovsky's impression of his first encounter with Diego Rivera in Mexico City. Such a description would have been much to Rivera's liking as it cultivated the image of a radical, larger-than-life Mexican revolutionary.

José Diego Maria Rivera was born on 13 December 1886, in the provincial town of Guanajuato, to educated parents of liberal views at a time when Mexico lay under the oppressive rule of President Porfirio Díaz. Although many intellectuals spoke out against the Díaz regime, censorship was strict and the penalties severe. Rivera's father expressed his radical views in the newspaper *El Democrata* and this led to his victimization. For this reason, in 1892, Diego and his family moved to live in the capital.

Rivera's parents had both worked as teachers and, not surprisingly, Diego did well at school showing an early aptitude for drawing. In December 1896, he enrolled at the evening art classes at the Academy of San Carlos – the leading art school in Mexico City. By the age of twelve, he had completed his elementary education and, at the insistence of his father, enrolled at a military college. The strict regime there, however, was little to his taste, and fortunately after only two weeks, he was awarded a scholarship to the San Carlos Academy and permitted to enrol in full-time art classes. He was to remain there for seven years and became one of the leading students.

By the time Rivera reached physical maturity, he had already acquired an imposing physique – weighing over 21 stone, he stood over six foot high. His appearance was quite extraordinary for, in addition to his gigantic size, he had twinkling, frog-like eyes and broad lips which would expand into a Buddha-like smile. His style of dress was flamboyant; he wore wide-brimmed hats, mining boots and enormous shirts. His generous build was matched by his equally larger-than-life personality, boundless energy and constant thirst for new experiences. He made friends easily and had numerous love affairs; he was also a wonderful story-teller and would relate elaborate, largely fictitious, tales about his life.

A precocious child
(below left) Diego had a passion and talent for drawing when very young. 'My earliest memory', he later recalled, 'is that I was drawing.'

Diego's birthplace
(below) Guanajuato was a Mexican city built on the wealth of silver mines, but these were almost worked out by the time Diego was born.

INBA/Desmond Rochfort

Ava Vargas

In January 1907, Rivera left Mexico for Madrid on a four-year scholarship to study European art. Two years later he moved to Paris, which was to become his home for the next 12 years, although he returned briefly to Mexico at the end of 1910 to exhibit some of his work. In Paris, he became one of the lions of the Montparnasse café society, forming close relations with leading avant-garde artists and writers; Modigliani, in particular, became a close friend. He set up house with Angeline Beloff, a Russian émigré artist, and in 1912, went with her to Toledo to work for the summer. There, the work of El Greco altered his attitude to colour and structure in painting.

JOINING THE CUBISTS

In his search for direction in his work, Rivera was constantly absorbing new influences. He became fascinated by the work of Cubist painters and Robert Delaunay's ideas about simultaneous representation of objects and events were of particular interest to him. In 1914, he met Juan Gris and encountered Picasso, who enthusiastically encouraged him in · his Cubist experiments. However, warm relations soon cooled when Picasso felt that one of Rivera's paintings was too close to one of his own. Nevertheless, Rivera maintained his friendship and artistic contact with another group of Cubists which included Juán Gris, Jacques Lipchitz and André Lhote. It was not until a prominent critic, Pierre Reverdy, publicly

Photo: The Detroit Institute of Arts/Dirk Bakker

Museo Diego Rivera, Guanajuato (INBA)

La Era
(above) Painted while Rivera was studying in Mexico City, this work shows the influence of his teacher Velasco, who taught perspective and loved Mexican landscape.

Collection of Marika Rivera Phillips

Homage to the friends of Montparnasse
(left) Rivera was part of the artistic community flourishing in Montparnasse in Paris in the early years of this century. This painting, by his mistress Marevna, shows their circle of friends: (back row) Rivera, Ehrenburg, Soutine, Jeanne Hébuterne, Max Jacob, Zborowsky; (front row) Marevna and her daughter, Marika, Modigliani and Kisling.

David Parker

Visit to the Yucatán
(left) Rivera toured the Yucatán in 1921 and was moved by the ruins at Uxmal. His sketches of the landscape and people later figured in his work.

Later that year Rivera married the writer Guadalupe Marin, a passionate and violent woman, by whom he had two daughters. He described her as a wild animal with 'transparent green eyes', 'animal teeth' and 'eagle talons'. The marriage was a stormy one and finally ended after Rivera's affairs with one of his models. Rivera attracted women like a magnet, as is described by Herrera, his second wife's biographer: 'Part of his appeal was his monstrous appearance – his ugliness made a perfect foil for the type of woman who likes to play beauty to a beast – but the greater attraction was his personality. He was a frog prince, an extraordinary man full of brilliant humour, vitality and charm. He could be tender and deeply sensuous'.

denounced Rivera's and Lhote's work in favour of the other members of the group that Rivera broke with his former friends, after coming to blows with Reverdy.

During this time, Rivera met another Russian emigré artist who was also experimenting with Cubism, Marevna Vorobëv-Stebelska. He became infatuated with her and left Angeline to live with her for a year in 1915. She refused to marry him as Angeline was, at the time, pregnant, but their affair lasted for another six years. They had a daughter, Marika, who was born in 1919; sadly, the son, Diego, born to Angeline, died of influenza during an epidemic at the age of two.

ART AND REVOLUTION

Politics came to assume a greater importance for Rivera around the time of the Russian Revolution and he became interested in the role that art could play in the service of society. At the suggestion of the Mexican Ambassador to France, Alberto J. Pani – who had started to buy his work – Rivera went to Italy to study the mural art of the Italian Renaissance, with a view to using this experience to establish a new post-revolutionary art in Mexico. He finally returned to his native country in the summer of 1921, leaving behind him Angeline, Marevna and his circle of friends.

A major programme of mural decoration on public buildings in Mexico had already been embarked upon, under the supervision of José Vasconcelos, Minister of Education. Rivera joined a group of artists and intellectuals that had just returned from Europe, to view the Indian sites in the Yucatán, in a familiarization programme led by Vàsconcelos intended to acquaint them with their pre-Conquest heritage. From this time, Pre-Columbian influences fused with pictorial conventions of the Renaissance in Rivera's work. In 1922, he began work on his first mural, *Creation*, in the National Preparatory School, Mexico City.

Photo: The Detroit Institute of Arts/Dirk Bakker

Museo de Arte Moderno, Mexico City (INBA)

'Los Tres Grandes'

The Mexican Mural Movement was a socio-political art movement that made history visual for the largely illiterate population of post-revolutionary Mexico. It was dominated by Los Tres Grandes (the 'Big Three') – Orozco, Siqueiros and Rivera. All three artists were first commissioned by Vasconcelos, Minister of Education, to do murals for the National Preparatory School and without any technical knowledge they sought to revive an art that had been dead for 400 years. They took their art to the USA during the years of political repression in the '30s.

National Preparatory School, Mexico City (INBA)

Desmond Rochfort

Jose Clemente Orozco (1883-1949)
(above) In The Trench, *Orozco uses the imagery of Christ and the Cross to express the sacrifices of the Mexican revolutionaries.*

David Alfaro Siqueiros (1896-1974)
(left) Siqueiros fought in the Mexican Revolution and the Spanish Civil War. In his work he was the most experimental of the muralists, using cement fresco and the spray gun, and choosing dramatic viewpoints and foreshortenings.

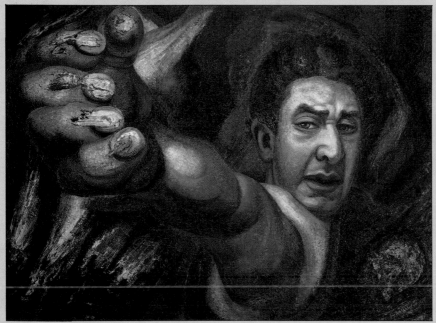

David Alfaro Siqueiros/Self-portrait/Museo de Arte Moderno, Mexico City (INBA)

Roland/Ziolo

Comitato Tina Modotti, Trieste

Diego's first wife
(left) Diego and the wild Guadalupe were married for 5 years. When pregnant, she modelled for the murals in the Chapingo chapel.

Political affiliations
(above) Diego was an active Communist and visited the Soviet Union in 1928, when he worked with a group of Moscow artists called 'Octobre'.

In March 1923, Rivera was commissioned to decorate the walls of Vasconcelos's own Ministry of Public Education – a project which was to take over four years of intensive work. When complete, the cycle comprised 117 fresco panels covering nearly 1,600 square metres. Before completing this cycle, Rivera embarked upon another set of murals for the chapel at the National School of Agriculture at Chapingo. The sheer scale of these murals made them exhausting to work on and Rivera frequently suffered from physical strain. 'Work was to him a kind of narcotic and any impediment to it irritated him . . . sometimes he laboured without stopping for days at a time, taking his meals on the scaffold and, if necessary, sleeping there'. It was in doing this that he seriously injured himself in 1927, when he fell from the scaffold at Chapingo and was knocked unconscious.

Rivera's political activities now became more intense; he was an active member of the Anti-Imperialist League of the Americas and was elected President of the Workers' and Farmers' Bloc, under whose auspices he was invited to attend the celebrations for the 10th anniversary of the October Revolution being held in Moscow in 1927. He remained active in the Mexican Communist Party until March 1929, when he began to dissociate himself from its Stalinist

111

Frida Kahlo

Frida Kahlo was born in 1907 in Coyoacán, a suburb of Mexico City. In 1925, an accident between a tram and a school bus left her with a crushed back, pelvis and leg, and she had to endure continual pain for the rest of her life. While she was in hospital, Frida began to paint. Most of her pictures were portraits of herself and celebrations of her suffering, as she explained: 'I paint myself because I am so often alone.' On her discharge from hospital she joined the Communist Party, and in 1929 she married Diego Rivera. Throughout the 1940s Frida fought against her failing health to retain her involvement in teaching and political activism. She died at her home in Coyoacán in 1954.

Frida and Diego, 1931
(right) *Frida's touching portrait – reminiscent of naive votive images – dates from two years after their wedding. She and Rivera were devoted to each other, but the marriage was a tempestuous one, marked by frequent infidelities and reconciliations.*

Frida at work in 1952
(below) *Despite living in Rivera's shadow, Frida established her own reputation as a highly original Surrealist artist.*

Gift of Albert M. Bender/San Francisco Museum of Modern Art

policies and openly anti-government stance. He was eventually expelled from the Communist Party for non-adherence to the Party line and switched his allegiance to Leon Trotsky.

In the summer of 1929, Rivera began work on the *History of Mexico* murals at the National Palace in Mexico; at the same time he married Frida Kahlo, a young artist. At twenty, Frida was half his age, but she became one of the most important factors in his life. Her appearance was striking for, in Rivera's own words, 'Her hair was long; dark and thick eyebrows met above her nose. They seemed like the wings of a blackbird, their black arches framing two extraordinary brown eyes'. Frida was also tiny and her parents said 'that it was like a marriage between an elephant and a dove'.

SUCCESS IN THE STATES

At the end of 1931, Rivera was in New York to attend a major retrospective of his work at the Museum of Modern Art. The exhibition was a phenomenal success with over 57,000 people passing through in four weeks. Rivera then travelled with Frida to Detroit, to prepare sketches in the massive Ford Rouge Plant for a large mural cycle on the theme of Detroit Industry, sponsored by Edsel B. Ford. This commission took ten months of intensive work to complete, with the help of seven assistants. Immediately after this, at

Gisèle Freund/The John Hillelson Agency

Photo: The Detroit Institute of Arts/Dirk Bakker

INBA

the invitation of the Rockefellers, Rivera moved to New York to execute a mural for the new RCA Building in Rockefeller Center.

This mural, entitled *Man at the Crossroads Looking with Hope and High Vision to the Choosing of a New and Better Future*, never saw completion. It had obviously not occurred to the young Nelson Rockefeller that a dedicated Communist might not be best suited to decorate one of the monuments to capitalist success. Indeed, when Rockefeller saw that Rivera had painted a portrait of Lenin into the mural, he requested that it should be removed; Rivera refused and was promptly taken off the job, paid the full amount of his commission and the uncompleted work was destroyed. A public outcry followed, but it was to no avail. On his return to Mexico in 1934, one of the first projects Rivera was to complete was a smaller version of this mural for the National Palace.

Rivera was extremely reluctant to leave the USA and was in low spirits and poor health when he arrived back in Mexico. A drastic diet had left him 'weak, thin, yellow and morally exhausted'. He continued to be widely criticized by former colleagues in the Communist Party, largely for his support for Trotsky. Rivera was, in fact, to play an active role in finding political asylum for Trotsky in Mexico and the Trotskys initially stayed with Rivera and Frida at their home at Coyoacán; they were joined for a time in 1938 by the Surrealists,

Rockefeller Controversy

Rivera intended his mural for the Rockefeller Center to be a celebration of humanity's advance through science and technology. But his vision of a worker's utopia that included Lenin caused a storm in the press, and Rockefeller ordered the mural's destruction. Rivera took his revenge in the later version of the fresco painted for the National Palace, Mexico (left) by placing Rockefeller's grandfather next to the syphilis bacteria in one of the ellipses.

Art and Politics

(below) Rivera is seen here talking to the French Surrealist writer André Breton and his wife Jacqueline, and Leon Trotsky. In 1938 the Riveras, the Bretons and the Trotskys went on a tour of Mexico, discussing art and politics as they went. The friendship had mixed blessings – Breton arranged a Paris exhibition for Frida, but her affair with Trotsky led to the Riveras' divorce.

André and Jacqueline Breton. However, Rivera's barely suppressed anarchism as well as Frida's affair with Trotsky, created considerable strains on their relationships, and in April 1939, Rivera and Trotsky reached a 'parting of the ways'. Shortly after this he and Frida divorced, although they were to remarry the following year.

Rivera continued to accept mural and portrait commissions throughout the 1940s and began construction of Anahuacalli, a massive stone-built 'temple' near Coyoacán which was to serve as house, museum and tomb; he worked on this project intermittently until his death, and it now houses his huge collection of Pre-Columbian art.

ONE LAST SCANDAL

In 1948, a final breath of scandal informed one of his last major works when he included the slogan 'God does not exist' in his panel *Dream of a Sunday Afternoon in the Alameda* (pp.128-9), destined for the foyer of the Hotel del Prado. The management refused to unveil the work and the mural was kept covered for nine years, until Rivera agreed to the removal of the offending words; this he did on his return from a trip in Eastern Europe, when he announced that he had become a Catholic.

Frida Kahlo died on 13 July 1954, and Rivera was heartbroken: 'It was the most tragic day of my life'. The next year he was informed that he had cancer, but he continued to work. Looking forward as ever, he married his dealer and set up a trust fund to administer Anahuacalli and Frida's Coyoacán home as museums after his death. At the end of 1955, he travelled to Moscow to undergo cobalt treatment and claimed he had been completely cured. He continued planning for future mural projects and was still painting at 70, when he died of a heart attack in his San Angel studio on 24 November 1957. He was buried with official honours, leaving his art to the nation.

Jacqueline Lambton Collection/Edimedia

Art for the Masses

Drawing on his knowledge of Pre-Columbian art, Rivera created a kaleidoscopic vision of Mexican civilisation, illustrating its progress towards revolution and a socialist future.

Photo: The Detroit Institute of Arts/Dirk Bakker

Museo Nacional de Arte Moderno, Mexico City (INBA)

he gave a series of lectures for fellow artists on Cézanne's methods of construction. This study of Cézanne's pictorial space and simplified forms, together with his meeting Juan Gris and Robert Delaunay, led Rivera to his first experiments with Cubism around 1913. He soon developed his own version of the style that was quite different to the work of the other Cubists, often incorporating Mexican motifs juxtaposed with areas of strong hard-edged colour.

Rivera broke with Cubism in 1917, and returned to his study of the work of Ingres and Renoir. During his 17 months in Italy, Rivera also became familiar with the fresco cycles of Giotto, Masaccio and Piero della Francesca. Significantly for the future of his work, he was particularly impressed by the organization of these large-scale murals into an architectural environment, and by their manipulation of perspective.

On his return to Mexico in 1921, Rivera at last found the cause for which he had been searching,

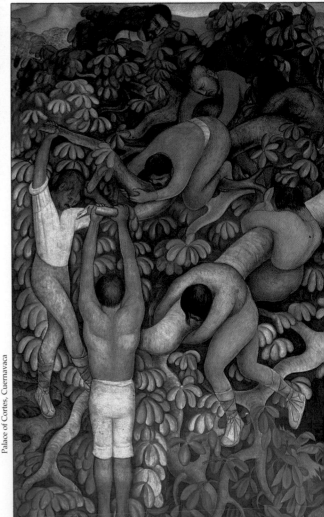

Rivera's first work at the San Carlos Academy consisted of competent studies of casts. His teacher, Santiago Rebull, a former student of Ingres, greatly influenced Rivera's drawing style and method of composition, providing him with a reverence for Classicism and a strong attachment to line that was to resurface in the great mural projects of the 1920s and 1930s. During his student days, the artist also became acquainted with the richness and beauty of Pre-Columbian art, which he was to collect so avidly in later life.

From the very start of his career, Rivera was interested in the latest developments in modern art, and during his 20s he rapidly assimilated the lessons of every contemporary art movement. The most enduring influence on his work was Cézanne, whose paintings so inspired Rivera that

Zapatista Landscape – The Guerilla (1915)
(above) During his early years in Paris, Rivera developed his own distinctive version of Cubism, which was decorative, highly coloured and often incorporated recognizable objects. Here, for example, the attributes of Zapata's peasant army – a sombrero, a Mexican shawl and a rifle – float against a Mexican landscape.

Palace of Cortes, Cuernavaca

The Peasant (1934)

(left) Rivera was a gifted draughtsman, and always carried a sketchbook with him to record his spontaneous observations. His watercolour and pencil sketches of Mexican peasants are remarkable for their simplicity and directness.

The Artist's Studio (1954)

(below) In this almost Surrealist work, Rivera portrays some of his sources of inspiration. Grotesque papier-maché dolls from Mexican Easter celebrations float menacingly above the reclining woman, while some favourite Pre-Columbian figures stand on the table.

Private Collection

when he began to see the role that his art could play in furthering the revolutionary cause. The trip to the Yucatán in 1921 and the visit to Tehuantepec in the following year, were also of immense importance to the artist, along with the general revival of interest in Mexican traditions.

For his first major fresco commission for the Ministry of Public Education, Rivera created a Cosmography of Modern Mexico. In 1,600 square metres of fresco panels, Rivera constructed a kaleidoscopic image of modern Mexico of extraordinary complexity. *The Corrido of the Agrarian Revolution* and *The Corrido of the Proletarian Revolution*, two major series within the work illustrate the revolutionary *corridos* or ballads. They show the savage faces of Imperialism and Capitalism set against the idealism of the Revolution and the simple life of the peasantry. Sumptuous colour harmonies are combined with a restrained classicism of form to give the impression of a continuous tableau frozen in the midst of action. In this way, the specific incidents that Rivera illustrates become part of a wider historical development.

While he was working at the Ministry of Education, Rivera embarked upon the most harmonious and architecturally integrated project

Crossing the Barranca (1930)

(below) This panel painted for the Palace of Cortes shows the Spaniards crossing a ravine (barranca) to battle with the Aztecs in the village of Cuernavaca.

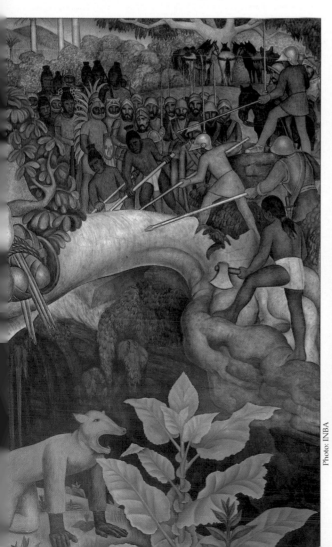

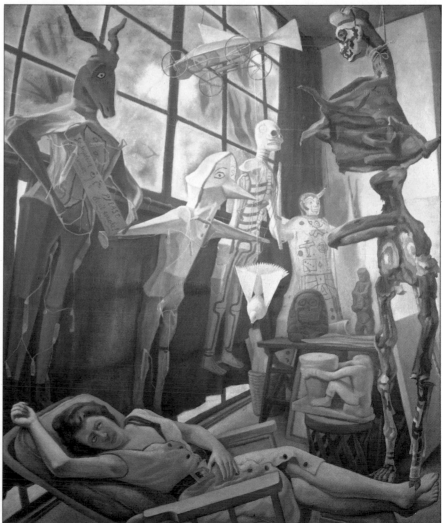

Museo Nacional de Arte Moderno, Mexico City (INBA)

115

The Tradition of Wall Painting

The tradition of wall painting as an essential expression of Mexican life and thought has continued unbroken since prehistoric times. Highly symbolic and often religious in character, Pre-Columbian murals such as those at Teotihuacan (450-650 AD) and Bonampak (692 AD) reveal great skill combined with a sophisticated sense of colour. After the conquest, the Spanish called on native artists to decorate the new churches until the Baroque period, when florid ornamentation became the vogue. Nevertheless, mural painting continued to flourish in popular art into the 20th century, decorating pulquerias, dairies, haciendas, mines and country churches.

A Pulqueria
(above) Traditional Mexican inns, known as pulquerias, *were frequently decorated with vivid scenes showing the preparation of the liquor pulque from the maguy cactus, comic episodes and landscapes. Many of these colourful scenes were whitewashed following the Revolution.*

The Bonampak murals (692 AD)
(left) The most famous Mayan murals are those at Bonampak, which were only discovered in 1946. They show a series of rituals and battles involving figure wearing crested helmets.

UNESCO/Ziolo

he was ever to complete the mural cycle *The Liberated Earth with Natural Forces Controlled by Man* (opposite). It was for the Chapel of the National School of Agriculture at Chapingo, just outside Mexico City. These murals illustrated the School's slogan 'Exploitation of the Land, not of Man' and dealt with the reconstruction of Mexico after the chaos of Revolution. As in the Education Ministry murals, Rivera sought to demonstrate the community of interest between worker and peasant in support of the revolutionary ideal of class struggle.

HISTORICAL THEMES

A year after his return from the Soviet Union, Rivera started work on the stairway of the National Palace in Mexico City with a panoramic view of *The History of Mexico: from the Conquest to the Future* (pp. 124-5). The Mexican history theme continued into the next major commission, the murals for the Palace of Cortez in Cuernavaca, which illustrated *The Battle of the Aztecs and the Spaniards* (pp. 114-15). At around this time Rivera was experiencing acute political difficulties, because although he had been expelled from the Communist party he was still widely perceived as a left-wing radical, and in an increasingly right-wing political climate, the opportunities for public commissions in Mexico were rapidly diminishing. But Rivera managed to find an outlet for his revolutionary zeal in the work he did in the United States.

Fascinated by machinery from childhood, the artist found his vision of the future realized in the most advanced methods of industrialization, and an idealized view of mass production and scientific processes now began to appear in his work. The most striking and ambitious of these projects were

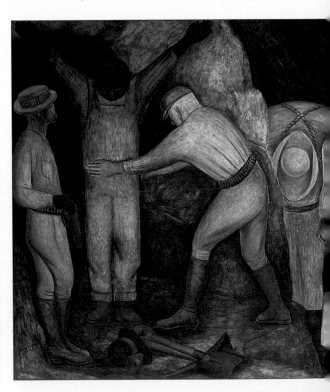

TRADEMARKS

Monumental Forms

The figures in Rivera's paintings give an impression of enduring solidity. The artist's practice of working on a large scale often led him to portray people as a series of massive rounded forms, and to eliminate clutter and detail in favour of a simple presentation and visual impact.

Photo: The Detroit Institute of Arts/Dirk Bakker

INBA

INBA

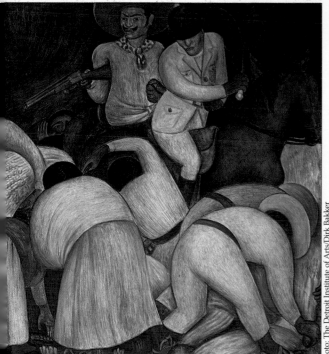

Photo: The Detroit Institute of Arts/Dirk Bakker

INBA

Chapingo Chapel (1926-7)

(above and left) Rivera's frescoes in the Chapel at the Agricultural School at Chapingo are remarkable for their rich saturated colours and their bold design. They portray the regeneration of Mexican agriculture both historically and symbolically. The panels on the right wall illustrate fertility and growth in Nature, while those on the left show agriculture transformed by social revolution. In The Formation of the Revolutionary Leadership *(left) a landowner and armed guards are shown as oppressors of the peons.*

the 27 fresco panels *Detroit Industry* (pp. 126-7), painted for the Detroit Art Institute during 1932 and 1933. Here River built upon the themes first developed at Chapingo to give an integrated view of the Universe in which men and women of all races, god-like machines and fertile Nature co-exist in harmony. Consciously monumental, the frescoes illustrate an ideal world dedicated to progress. Many of the machines have symmetrical forms which are reminiscent of the sculptures of the ancient Aztec gods which Rivera so admired.

Rivera continued to use traditional forms to portray a utopian and sometimes naive view of the world for the rest of his career, while at the same time experimenting with new ideas and techniques. In *The History of Medicine in Mexico* (pp. 130-31) for example, in which traditional and modern healing arts are presented side by side, heightened colour and compressed space are combined with a huge traditional representation of Tlazoltéotl, the Aztec goddess of childbirth and cleanliness. This extraordinary ability to fuse the old and the new together with the sheer scope of Rivera's work, makes the artist the giant of modern Mexican painting.

THE MAKING OF A MASTERPIECE

Rivera's magnificent fresco in the National Palace, *The History of Mexico from the Conquest to the Future*, was painted in two places, from 1929-30 and in 1935. It is located on the main wall over the grand sweep of the entrance stairway, and presented as a five-year pageant of historical personalities and periods. In the centre, Rivera has depicted an enormous heraldic eagle, representing the foundation of the Aztec Empire – on the site of modern Mexico City. Below, the Spanish invaders, led by Hernan Cortés, are engaged in fierce hand-to-hand combat with the Mexican Indians. The other episodes illustrated include the destruction of the pagan temples by Cortés after the Conquest, the tyranny of the Holy Inquisition, the fight for Mexican independence, the two foreign invasions of Mexico, and the Mexican Revolution of 1910.

Mexican Independence
(left) At the centre of his compressed and kaleidoscopic view of Mexican civilization, Rivera has shown the eagle, symbol of Mexico's pride and strength, clutching the Aztec symbol of war in its beak. Above, under the revolutionary slogan of 'Land and Liberty', stands the figure of Don Miguel Hidalgo, holding the chains of slavery, who led the fight for Mexican Independence. He is surrounded by three of his most formidable generals – an aristocrat, a priest and a peasant.

The Holy Inquisition
(right) In this episode, Rivera graphically depicts an auto da fé *– the Inquisition's public punishment for heretics.*

Photo: The Detroit Institute of Arts/Dirk Bakker

INBA

The Huastec Civilization
(right) *A second cycle of 11 fresco panels 'From Prehistoric Civilization to the Conquest' was added between 1945 and 1951, on the second floor.*

Bridgeman Art Library

INBA

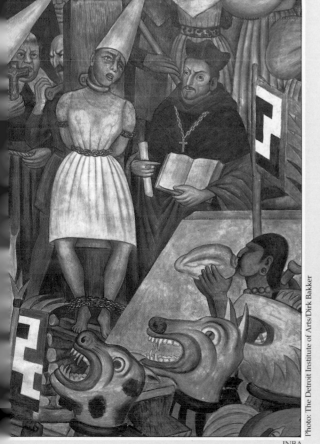

Photo: The Detroit Institute of Arts/Dirk Bakker

INBA

'Mexican mural painting made the masses the hero of monumental art.'

Diego Rivera

Ancient sources
(below) *Rivera drew heavily on images from Pre-Columbian art. The banner, for example, in* The Huastec Civilization, *is copied from a ceremonial platform in the Codex Borbonicus.*

Bibliothèque de l'Assemblée Nationale, Paris

Rivera's prodigious output forms one of the most overwhelming achievements in modern art. Covering vast areas of wall with teeming multi-figure compositions, Rivera deployed his formidable energy and seemingly inexhaustible imagination on themes expressing his fervent political views – the destruction of capitalism, the eradication of

Our Bread *1923-28*
80¼″ × 62¼″ Ministry of Education, Mexico City

This and the painting opposite are part of Rivera's first great mural scheme, Corrido (song) of the Proletarian Revolution, *involving 116 fresco compositions in the Ministry of Education building. Here, Rivera links Communism, in the form of the provider at the head of the table, with the supply of food, as representatives of the Mexican nation look on in reverential gratitude.*

E.T. Archive

INBA

poverty and social injustice, and the triumph of the Mexican people through creative labour. In his early murals at the Ministry of Education, Rivera worked in a comparatively naturalistic style, each panel forming an independent picture, but he soon developed a more complex, richly layered manner in which past and present mingle and

traditional ideas of scale and space are often abandoned in the cause of greater expressiveness and pictorial splendour.

Although Rivera's name is inseparable from the heroic part he played in the revival of monumental mural painting, he was also a superb easel painter, as is seen in The Grinder and Flower Seller.

E.T. Archive

INBA

Protest *1923-8*
80¼" × 66¼" Ministry of Education, Mexico City

Rivera's murals in the Court of Labour and the Court of the Fiestas in the Ministry of Education present a richly-varied view of post-revolutionary Mexico, depicting the life, revolutionary history and aspirations of the people.

In Protest, men vote unanimously over an unseen resolution while a flag bearing the emblems of the USSR flies before the smoking chimneys of industry.

121

The Grinder *1924*
35½″ × 46″ Museo de Arte Moderno, Mexico City

*Rivera knew Picasso in Paris and occasionally his paintings come close
in form and spirit to the work of the great Spaniard. This massively
simple figure is an example, being reminiscent of Picasso's 'classical'
work of the same period and making an heroic image out of everyday
life. The woman is making tortillas – the maize pancakes that are a
staple part of the Mexican diet.*

Flower Seller *1926*
35¼″ × 43¼″ Honolulu Academy of Arts

*As in the painting on the opposite page, Rivera here paints with
inspired boldness and vigour. Whereas* The Grinder, *however, is
done in encaustic (a technique using hot, coloured wax that was
common in the ancient world and has been revived sporadically since),
in this canvas Rivera splendidly exploits the colouristic richness of the
oil medium. Note the child feeding at its mother's breast.*

History of Mexico: From the Conquest to the Future *1929-30 and 1935*
Approximately 28′ high in centre of main wall
National Palace, Mexico City

The National Palace which houses these impressive murals is the seat of the President of the Republic of Mexico, its foundations rising from the ruins of the ancient Aztec royal palace. The frescoes are part of a huge scheme covering Mexico's history from the fall of Teotihuacan in about 900 AD to Rivera's own time. The stairway murals begin with the Spanish Conquest, and the earlier history is covered in a series of frescoes that run round the open gallery (surrounding a courtyard) to

which the stairway leads. Although the stairway walls were painted with Rivera's customary speed, the rest of the scheme (originally intended to occupy all four sides of the courtyard) was left unfinished at his death in 1957. At the centre of the entire composition, on the west wall, is an eagle, the national symbol of Mexico. This wall represents events from the Conquest to 1930 and includes some ferocious scenes of combat. The north wall (shown lower right) features the Aztec World, and the south wall (shown lower left) Mexico Today and Tomorrow. Rivera painted this wall in 1935 after a break to undertake various projects in the United States. At the top is a figure of 'Karl Marx pointing to the utopia that awaits the abolition of social classes'.

Dirk Bakker

Detroit Industry (south wall)
1932-33
Main panel 17′8″ × 45′
Detroit Institute of Arts

The commission for this fresco cycle – Rivera's most ambitious work in the United States – was given to the artist by William R. Valentiner, the Director of the Institute, after the two men had met in San Francisco in 1930. Originally Rivera was asked to paint only two panels, which he planned to devote to the automobile industry for which the city is famous. However, as he began touring the city and making sketches, Rivera's enthusiasm for the project grew, and he had little difficulty in persuading the museum's governing board to expand his commission to include the whole of the court – 27 panels of varying size. The main panel of this wall is devoted to the car industry and shows various stages in the production of a car. Above, the reclining figures represent the yellow and white races (the red and black races are on the opposite wall). The upper corner panels represent the pharmaceutical (left) and commercial chemical (right) industries; below them the small panels depict a surgical operation (left) and crystallized sulphur and potash (right). All these disparate elements are moulded by Rivera into a marvellous decorative whole, the problems of filling the awkward shapes created by the architectural setting solved brilliantly. The monumental stamping press to the right of the composition echoes the massive sculpture of Coatlicue, the pre-Columbian Aztec Earth Mother now in the Anthropological Museum in Mexico City.

Dream of a Sunday Afternoon in the Alameda *1947-48*
15'8" × 49' Alameda, Mexico City

*This huge fresco presents an extraordinary diversity of characters in a
sequence that reads chronologically from left to right. The Alameda
Park is the most popular place in Mexico City for a Sunday afternoon
stroll, and Rivera has used the setting to depict a representative
cross-section of Mexican history and society. Many of the figures are
historical personages, four of them – because of their importance in
Mexican history – being depicted on a larger scale than the others,
notably Emiliano Zapata on the rearing horse to the right. Others are
representatives of types, such as the boy pickpocket near the extreme
left. The figure in the centre with the bowler hat and cane is José
Guadalupe Posada, the artist whose political caricatures were
immensely popular and who became a great influence on 20th-century
Mexican art. He stands next to a calavera or animated skeleton, one
of the recurring themes of his work, and the child standing next in line
is a portrait of Rivera himself as a boy. Behind the boy stands Rivera's
second wife, Frida Kahlo. Originally in the Hotel del Prado, the
fresco was moved to its present, specially built site after the
earthquake of 1985.*

Photo: The Detroit Institute of Arts/Dirk Bakker

The History of Medicine in Mexico: The People's demand for Better Health *1953*
approximately 24' × 35'
Hospital de la Raza,
Mexico City

This fresco is a celebration of medical science, past and present, in Mexico's leading national hospital. As in many of his works, Rivera combines historical and contemporary images, here representing Pre-Columbian medical practice contrasted with the latest scientific solutions. The dominant central motif, which he took from a 16th-century Indian codex (manuscript volume), is the figure of Tlazoltéotl, the Aztec goddess of cleanliness, who was seen as a guardian of childbirth. Rivera's powerful sense of design enabled him to combine without any sense of incongruity this stylized image with the vividly naturalistic scenes all around.

The Mexican Revolution

The Revolution of 1910-20 marked the beginning of Mexico's painful quest for her own identity as a nation after four centuries of political, cultural and social repression.

In 1910, the Mexican President Porfirio Díaz – a virtual dictator – could look back and congratulate himself on 35 years of peace and growing prosperity. But it had been won at tremendous cost: for bringing Mexico into the 20th century required considerable foreign investment in mining, as well as the construction of thousands of kilometres of railroad. Meanwhile, the gradual breakup of the Indian *ejidos*, or common lands, had given rise to the *hacienda* system of vast estates manned by 'peons' (Indian labourers) in virtual debt slavery. Miners were equally disaffected and occasional strikes broke out which were put down brutally. Díaz despised the Indians and maintained a stranglehold on the populace by the repressive use of *'pan o palo'* (bread or the stick) administered by political bosses.

This authoritarian régime was morally sanctioned by a group of intellectuals enamoured of European culture, the *científicos*. Disciples of positivist philosophers such as Auguste Comte and Herbert Spencer, they advocated progress through scientific method and forward planning – to the benefit of the middle and moneyed classes. However, no one, least of all Díaz, had planned for the events of the next decade.

PRELUDE TO A REVOLUTION

In 1908, Díaz had made the major mistake of announcing his refusal to stand for re-election in 1910. Burgeoning opposition to the dictatorial régime seized on this, in particular, one Francisco I. Madero, heir to a substantial *hacienda*, who had founded a reform movement in his native state of Coahuila. In 1909, he published *The Presidential Succession in 1910*, in which he castigated the régime mercilessly. However, Díaz had no intention of resigning. On hearing of the president's intention to stand again, Madero founded the Anti-re-electionist party and canvassed for the presidency himself. Díaz had him imprisoned on a false charge, just before the elections in July 1910. Madero responded with the

Madero enters Mexico city
(above) On 7 June 1911, the reformer turned revolutionary, Francisco I. Madero entered Mexico city in triumph. President Díaz, who had fled the country shortly before, was reputed to have observed perceptively that 'Madero has unleashed a tiger, now let's see if he can control it'.

The age of Díaz
(left) This satirical view of the Porfiriato *by Siqueiros presents the ageing president trampling on the constitution surrounded by his cronies, the hated científicos.*

David Alfaro Siqueiros/The Díaz Dictatorship/Museo Nacional de Historia, Chapultepec Castle, Mexico City

Desmond Rochfort

Plan of San Luis Potosí, declaring the elections void, himself as provisional president and calling for an armed uprising on 20 November.

The revolt seemed to backfire at first, when disparate uprisings throughout the country were quelled. Madero fled to the US, but he had not reckoned with the support of the bandit leaders, Pascual Orozco and Pancho Villa – 'the Mexican Robin Hood'. These two recruited a rebel army that came to be known as the Division of the North, composed of men for whom an honourable death fighting for freedom was infinitely preferable to their impoverished slavery. Another rebellion arose in Morelos in the south, headed by Emiliano Zapata with the rallying call of *'Tierra y Libertad'* (Land and Liberty). Throughout the revolution, he would continually fight for the

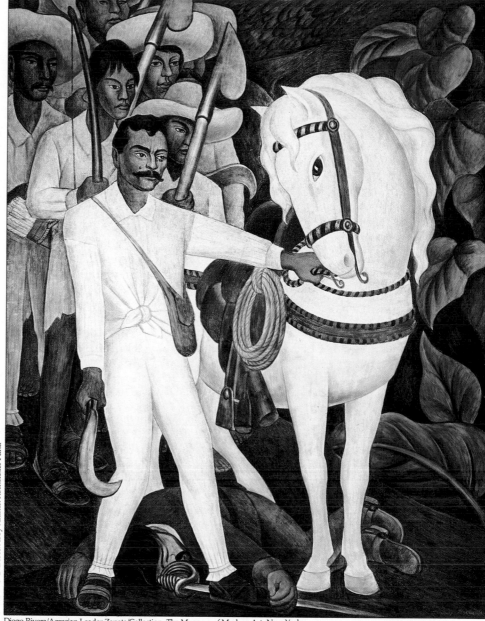

Diego Rivera/Agrarian Leader Zapata/Collection, The Museum of Modern Art, New York

7' 9¾" × 6' 2"/fresco/Abby Aldrich Rockefeller Fund

Revolutionary hero
(right) A copy of his mural at Cuernavaca, capital of Zapata's native state of Morelos, Rivera's painting of the leader of the south is a gentle portrait of the man who for nine years campaigned for 'Land and Liberty'.

Pancho Villa
(below) The unpredictable and brilliant commander of the Division of the North has been aptly described as 'a 20th-century compound of Attila the Hun, Robin Hood and Jesse James with a flavouring of red-hot chilli sauce'.

Bildarchiv Preussischer Kulturbesitz

BBC Hulton Picture Library

restoration of the Indian *ejidos* until his murder in 1919. 'Men of the south', he declared, 'it is better to die on your feet than live on your knees'.

By June 1911, Villa and Orozco had taken Ciudad Juarez and held the north. Díaz, in the face of violent demonstrations, finally resigned and fled to Paris, leaving the field free for Madero's return. A sincere, if not ingenuous man, Madero believed that with Díaz's removal, democracy would hold sway. Compromise proved his undoing, as Zapata once again raised the flag of revolt, demanding radical agrarian reform in his Plan of Ayala. Madero, forced to take action, made the unwise choice of calling on the hard-drinking and ambitious General Huerta.

BITTER POWER STRUGGLES

The story then took on the dimensions of a tragic farce: Orozco turned against Madero and found himself pitted against his former *compañero* Villa, who was allied with the army boss Huerta, who, in his turn, nearly had Villa executed. Meanwhile,

General Huerta
(left) Posada's calavera (skull caricature) of Huerta as a spider crushing the bones of his victims attacked the President's unbridled use of political assassination. Huerta also muzzled the press, employed spies and filled state jails with political prisoners.

Las Soldaderas
(right) Women played an essential role during the Revolution. They would accompany husbands or lovers, forage for food, act as cook, laundress and porter, as well as nurse the wounded. Sometimes they would even fight alongside the men, earning the title of soldadera.

Historic meeting
(below) Villa and Zapata finally met on 4 December 1914 at Xochimilco. Two days later they rode the 12 miles into Mexico City and were photographed seated in state in the National Palace. However, their mutual dislike of Carranza did not lead to military co-operation.

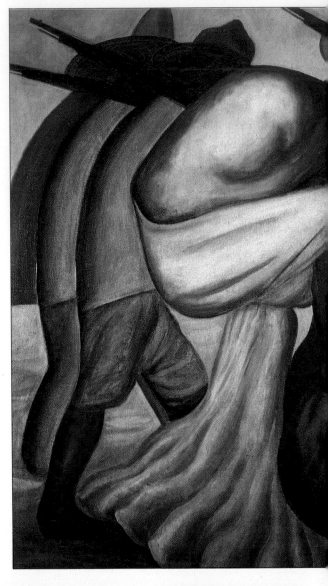

Felix Díaz, nephew of the ex-dictator, took Veracruz, joining up with another *Porfiriato* general, Bernardo Reyes. Both were captured and imprisoned in Mexico City, but succeeded in freeing themselves with the aid of the army. Díaz then took refuge in the city. Huerta secretly deserted Madero to make common cause with Díaz, and for ten days – the *Decena Trágica* – the capital became the scene of bloody carnage as the treacherous Huerta ostensibly bombarded Díaz and his rebel forces. But on the tenth day, Madero was forced to resign at gunpoint and he and his vice-president, Pino Suarez, were shot 'while they were trying to escape'.

HUERTA UNDER FIRE

Huerta had become president, but he was a reactionary and his government was soon under attack as a result of the murders of Madero and his vice-president. Venustiano Carranza, governor of Madero's native state of Coahuila, started a new uprising backed by Alvaro Obregón in Sonora and Villa in Chihuahua. The northern states again became the scene of guerilla warfare as government *federales* fought these rebels, while Zapata remained at large in Morelos. The situation was further complicated by American interference. The new President, Woodrow Wilson, who was strongly anti-Huerta, ordered the American occupation of Veracruz in response to an alleged insult. With his main port on the Caribbean blockaded, Huerta was isolated. He surrendered the Presidency on 15 July 1914 and fled to Spain.

All the revolutionary factions met that autumn at the Convention of Aguas Calientes, the aptly named, 'hot waters', where a clear split appeared between the Villistas and Zapatistas on one side and the Carrancistas and Obregón on the other. Indeed, dislike was sufficiently strong on Villa's part for him to suggest that he and Carranza take part in a joint suicide pact. A provisional president

Jose Clemente Orozco/Las Soldaderas/Museo Nacional de Arte Moderno, Mexico City

was elected, but Carranza, who was not prepared to step down, retreated to Veracruz as the Americans pulled out. Obregón withdrew from the capital, leaving it open to Villa and Zapata, the two great heroes of the revolution, who finally met on 4 December. After creating mayhem, both leaders left for their old battlegrounds and Obregón returned to milk the capital dry before setting after Villa and inflicting a crushing defeat on Villa's army at Celaya, with the aid of barbed wire and trench warfare, in April 1915. The Carranza regime was recognized by America, and in response, Villa spent the next few years taking reprisals against US citizens. He was harried, in turn, by an American punitive expedition under General Pershing.

Carranza had meanwhile consolidated his position in the capital and agreed to a congress at Queretaro to draw up a new constitution in 1916. His original mild document was transformed by the ideas of a young and dominant radical group backed by Obregón. The powers of the church were limited and primary education was declared both free and obligatory. Article 27 established

state ownership of all land and foreign owners had to accede to Mexican law. All *ejido* lands taken during the *Porfiriato* were to be returned and any additional lands were to be taken from private hands. Article 123 called for an eight-hour workday in a six-day week with a minimum wage and equal pay. Debt peonage was abolished, as was child labour, and compensation was demanded for industrial injuries.

THE NEW REGIME

The new Constitution of 1917 was an enlightened document, but Carranza, who won the elections in March, put little effort into its enforcement. Zapata and Villa were still at large, an embarrassment to the new régime. Zapata was tricked and assassinated, but Villa survived, eventually retiring to a *hacienda* at government expense. The President's interference in the free elections of 1920 led to a new revolt, headed by Obregón. Forced to flee, Carranza lingered to collect booty, even to the extent of stripping light fixtures from the National Palace, and was murdered on his way to Veracruz.

On 5 September 1920, Alvaro Obregón was elected President. His term and those after it were not to be free from dissension, but his genuine and realistic attempt to implement the new constitution marked a new, constructive phase in a revolution which, some say, still continues to this day. Moreover, his appointment of José Vasconcelos, a leading intellectual of the Revolution, as Minister of Education was a stroke of genius: 1000 village schools were established throughout Mexico between 1920-4. And his creation and backing of the mural programme, inspired by the revolution, became the vanguard, despite the overlay of Marxian dialectic, of what has been described as the Mexican Renaissance.

The Liberation of the Peon
(below) This tragic scene by Rivera reminds us that freedom for the Mexican peasant was only possible through death or revolution. The painting is a copy of a fresco from the vast series he painted in the Ministry of Public Education (1923-8). Its companion piece is a scene entitled The Village Schoolteacher *in which a mounted revolutionary stands guard as a teacher instructs a small group of Mexican villagers; a reminder that education in remote areas had been made possible by the Revolution.*

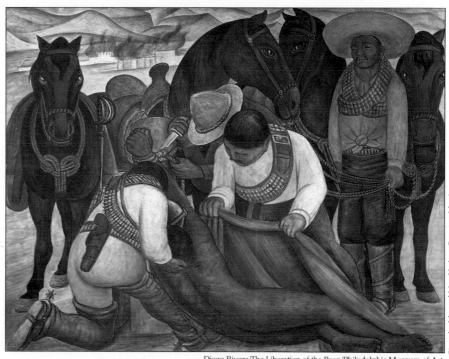

Diego Rivera/The Liberation of the Peon/Philadelphia Museum of Art

A Year in the Life 1921

When Rivera returned to his native Mexico, Europe, like his own country, was still recovering from years of war and revolution; Germany was staggering under the heavy burden of reparations, while in Soviet Russia, the Bolsheviks emerged triumphant but were threatened with devastating economic problems.

Rivera left behind a Europe still busily signing and scrapping agreements in the wake of the First World War. The knottiest problem of all was the payment of reparations, the money the victorious Allies hoped to extort from a 'war guilty' Germany to cover the entire cost of the conflict. In 1921, this sum was fixed at a fantastic 132 billion gold marks. According to the Allies, Germany had already fallen behind in her payments; consequently in January the French occupied three industrial cities of the Ruhr to force her hand. The Germans had no alternative but to agree to the Allied terms, although the future was to show that these were hopelessly unrealistic. Continuing Allied pressure led to the two-year occupation of the area in 1923 and was directly responsible for the collapse of the mark.

The Treaty of Versailles had left the major part of Poland's

Max Ernst/Celebes/Tate Gallery, London

© SPADEM 1988

The Cairo Conference

(above) At the beginning of 1921, Winston Churchill was appointed British Colonial Secretary with the additional responsibility of sorting out the Middle East after the chaos left in the wake of the Turkish collapse. He soon organized a team of experts (including Gertrude Bell and T. E. Lawrence) which met at Cairo in March. The key decision of the conference was to hand over Iraq to Feisal, leader of the Arab Revolt, so as to maintain indirect British rule over the strategic oil-rich state which had revolted against the Anglo-Indian administration only the year before.

Surreal Monster

(above) Max Ernst (1891-1976) began his artistic career in 1916 and soon rejected Expressionism in favour of the Dadaist anti-art movement. Ernst's study of psychology and fascination with the unconscious led him to use a variety of images with which he created dreamlike juxtapositions. Célèbes, shown here, was painted in 1921. In this extraordinary painting an elephantine creature with a bull's head confronts a headless but gloved nude in a landscape whose very context appears ambivalent – fish seem to swim in the sky.

Ceremonial inauguration

(right) The Northern Ireland parliament was inaugurated in June 1921 by George V. Unionists gained the majority of the seats just as Sinn Fein controlled the Dail Eireann or National Assembly of the Irish Republic in the south. The lines of division in Ireland were becoming more sharply marked.

borders undefined. A plebiscite in Upper Silesia showed that the majority of the population wished to remain German. Poland refused to accept this, since Germany had sent in over 200,000 'emigrant' voters, while 40% of the qualified residents abstained from voting. Insurrection broke out on 3 May, followed by six weeks fighting between Polish forces and German irregulars; ultimately Allied arbiters partitioned the province, awarding Poland the lion's share. In 1920, the Poles had also tried to seize the Ukraine in a counter offensive against the belligerence of the Red Army who were attempting to liberate revolutionary Germany and Poland. A Polish-Soviet peace treaty was concluded on 18 March 1921 at Riga.

After three years of civil war and interventions by Britain and other powers, the Bolsheviks had emerged triumphant.

Economic collapse and famine threatened, and the naval mutiny at Kronstadt – once a Bolshevik stronghold – convinced Lenin that he would have to rethink his policy of requisition. The introduction of the New Economic Policy (NEP) meant that peasants could sell their surplus produce for a profit, and a considerable degree of private enterprise was allowed to function in the Soviet cities.

TURMOIL IN IRELAND

In Ireland, rebellion, independence and civil war followed one another in quick succession. Officially and unofficially, the war between Sinn Fein and the British government had been going on since late 1919, greatly embittered during 1920 by the

BBC Hulton Picture Library

Controversial novelist
(left) D. H. Lawrence's novel Women in Love, *considered by many critics to be his finest, was not published in his native Britain until 1921 by Martin Secker, who, unlike other publishers, was prepared to risk prosecution. The Rainbow (1915) had been suppressed as obscene, but* Women in Love *escaped prosecution.*

Strong-arm tactics
(below) This German poster of defiance against the Belgian and French army of occupation in the Ruhr dates from 1923. However, two years before, the French, dissatisfied with Germany's inadequate reparations payments after the war, took the law into their own hands and invaded three German industrial towns in the Ruhr.

National Portrait Gallery, London

Nein!

Mich zwingt Ihr nicht!

Archiv für Kunst und Geschichte

Crispin Rodwell

Stormont Castle, Belfast

introduction of the government volunteer force, the notorious 'Black and Tans'. In July 1921 a truce was agreed, but the intransigent republican Éamon de Valera refused to accept Lloyd George's offer of Dominion status. Five months later, in de Valera's absence, Arthur Griffiths and Michael Collins accepted not only Dominion status for the proposed Irish Free State, but also the effective partition of Ireland separating Protestant Ulster from the Free State. By one of the ironies of history, one of the earliest actions of the first independent Irish government was to fight a bitter civil war using British artillery against the rejectionists led by de Valera.

In 1921, the Turkish nationalists under Mustapha Kemal were fighting for survival against an invading Greek army. There were anti-British riots in Egypt and India too was in turmoil, with risings against landlords and moneylenders and clashes between Hindus and Moslems; Gandhi launched his first civil disobedience campaign, but violence was to continue undiminished. However, the most successful anti-colonialists of 1921 were the Moroccan Rifs, who inflicted such a humiliating defeat on the Spaniards that their general committed suicide.

The same year that the British biographer Lytton Strachey published *Queen Victoria*, the first public edition of D. H. Lawrence's notorious *Women in Love* appeared, with extensive cuts. The year 1921 also saw the first performance of Prokofiev's delightful opera *The Love of Three Oranges* and, sadly, the death of Camille Saint-Saens, perhaps best known for his composition, *The Carnival of Animals*.

Jean-Loup Charmet

British rule under attack
(left) The Government of India Act of 1921 was passed as it was considered time that responsible self-government was introduced in the subcontinent, but only as an integral part of the British Empire. However, Indian participation in the war, the shock waves created by the Amritsar massacre of 1919 and not least a burgeoning sense of nationalism, created an atmosphere of antipathy and discontent with the British Raj. The time was ripe for Mohandas Gandhi to begin his campaign of peaceful non-cooperation with the Raj. In the autumn of 1921, he addressed a crowd of 60,000 only a short distance from where the Prince of Wales landed on a royal visit. However, this peaceable demonstration against British rule flared into violence. Although the Bombay riot soon quietened and Gandhi was imprisoned a few months later, the Raj would never be the same again. India was on the long road to independence.

The Kronstadt Rising
(below) The increasing discrepancies between the promises of the Bolshevik party and their performance led to the revolt of sailors of the Baltic fleet based at Kronstadt. After a failed infantry attack across the ice on 3 March, a second assault was launched against the rebels a fortnight later. By the following day the fighting had escalated into a massacre and the uprising was quashed.

Novosti Press Agency

GALLERY GUIDE

Hogarth

The best selection of Hogarth's work is to be found in London. There are major paintings in both the National Gallery and the Tate Gallery. However, Hogarth's satirical style is better represented in the smaller museums: the Coram Foundation, which the artist helped to set up, owns a number of canvases, while Sir John Soane's Museum features two of the best-known series, *The Rake's Progress* and *The Election*. In addition, Hogarth's attempts at history painting can be seen at St Bartholomew's Hospital and at Lincoln's Inn. Outside London, there are samples of the artist's work at Cambridge, Bristol and Liverpool. In America, Washington, New York and Philadelphia own some portraits, while the Albright-Knox Art Gallery in Buffalo possesses a fine example of the Englishman's moralizing approach.

Courbet

The majority of Courbet's most important works are in France. In Paris, the Musée d'Orsay contains his principal masterpiece, *The Painter's Studio, The Burial at Ornans* and *The Spring* and the Petit Palais also houses a fine selection of his pictures. Elsewhere in France, the Musée Fabre, Montpellier, now owns the collection assembled by Alfred Bruyas (p.48). There are a number of paintings at Bresançon, Lille, Caen, Nantes and the artist's native Ornans. In America, the best collection is at the Metropolitan Museum of Art, New York, which features the beautiful *Woman with a Parrot, Young Ladies of the Village* and a portrait of Jo Heffernan, who was Whistler's mistress. The Barnes Foundation (Merion, Pennsylvania), the Art Institute of Chicago and the Toledo Museum of Art also have striking examples of Courbet's talents.

Toulouse-Lautrec

The most comprehensive collection of the artist's work is at the Musée Toulouse-Lautrec, in Albi, and the Musée d'Orsay, Paris, also has a fine selection. Elsewhere in Europe, depictions of brothels can be found in Budapest and in the Tate Gallery, London; and there are notable portraits in Copenhagen (Ny Carlsberg Glyptotek) and in London (Courtauld Institute). In America, there are major works in Chicago and Philadelphia, while the Wadsworth Athenaeum, Hartford, and the Cleveland Museum of Art contain remarkable portraits. In addition, the Whitney Collection, New York, and the National Gallery of Art, Washington, possess paintings which illustrate the seamier side of Parisian night-life.

Rivera

Rivera's major mural schemes are situated in Mexico and the United States. His early, post-Revolutionary works include the *Creation*, at the National Preparatory School, Mexico City, his allegories at Chapingo Chapel, and the epic, historical schemes at the National Palace and at the Palace of Cortés, in Cuernavaca. Later, he produced more murals in Mexico City, notably at the Palace of Fine Arts, the Hotel Reforma, the Hotel del Prado (now at the Alameda), and the National Institute of Cardiology. The same city also provided Rivera's most unusual commission, at the Lerma Water-works, where the artist's designs were built around a massive, outdoor relief of the Rain God, Tláloc. In the United States, his most important work is the scheme at the Detroit Institute of Arts, although fine examples can be found in San Francisco (Pacific Stock Exchange and Institute of Art), and New York (New Workers School).

BIBLIOGRAPHY

D. Bindman, *Hogarth*, Thames and Hudson, New York, 1985
A. Bownes (intro), *Gustave Courbet 1819-77*, Exhibition Catalogue, Arts Council, London, 1978
A. Callen, *Courbet*, Hippocrene Books, New York, 1981
Detroit Institute of Arts, *Diego Rivera: a Retrospective* Norton, New York, 1986
A. Hauser, *The Social History of Art*, Random House, New York, 1985
J. Lassaigne, *Toulouse-Lautrec and the Paris of the Cabarets*, Lamplight Publishing, New York, 1975
L. Nochlin, *Realism*, Penguin Books, New York, 1972
R. Paulson, *Hogarth, His Life, Art and Times*, Yale University Press, New Haven, 1974
M. Rosenthal, *Hogarth*, Hippocrene Books, New York, 1981
V. Stewart, *45 Contemporary Mexican Artists*, Stanford University Press, Stanford, 1952
B. D. Wolfe, *The Fabulous Life of Diego Rivera*, Stein and Day, New York, 1984

OTHER SOCIAL COMMENTATORS

James Gillray/British Museum

which this had appeared, was suppressed in 1835 and Daumier was obliged to join the less vitriolic Charivari. He worked on this publication for most of his career, producing a wealth of satirical prints on the full range of bourgeois Parisian society, most notably on the legal profession. During his lifetime, Daumier was known only for these lithographs, but he was also a superb painter and his scenes of travellers and refugees betray a penetrating and sympathetic insight. His masterpieces in this vein were the depictions of a shabby group of itinerant players, the precursors of Picasso's tragic clowns. Daumier's career was cut short by blindness and only the kindness of Corot, who gave him a cottage, saved him from utter destitution.

Otto Dix (1891-1969)

German painter, a leading exponent of the Neue Sachlichkeit style. Dix trained in Dresden, before serving at the Front during the War. His experiences there dominated his early subject-matter, culminating in The Trench, a horrific, corpse-filled scene executed with merciless realism. Despite Dix's protests, this was seen by the authorities as an attack on German militarism and the picture was later confiscated by the Nazis. From the late 1920s, he turned his attention to the squalor of Berlin night-life and, in particular, to the local prostitutes, who seemed to epitomize the moral decay of the Weimar Republic. Dix's work was included in the 'Degenerate Art' exhibition (1937) and during World War II he maintained a low profile, concentrating on landscapes.

Gustave Doré (1832-83)

French illustrator and sculptor. Doré showed an early talent for lithography and, while still a schoolboy, was producing caricatures for Le Journal pour Rire. Rapidly, however, he started designing wood engravings, and by his early twenties his reputation was established. Doré's name was made by his illustrations to Balzac, Dante and Rabelais, in which he demonstrated a powerful, often macabre style. He was, however, equally capable of a shocking realism. His popularity in London – there was a Doré Gallery in Bond Street, which maintained a permanent exhibition of his work – brought him over to England each year. Here, in the 1870s, he produced a famous series of views highlighting, in horrifying detail, the wretchedness of the city's slums. Towards the end of his career, he turned to sculpture.

James Gillray (1757-1815)

The greatest English caricaturist. Gillray grew up in London where his father, an ex-soldier, worked as a sexton. He was briefly apprenticed to an engraver, but abandoned this to join a group of travelling players. Then in 1778 he entered the Royal Academy Schools, where he was a contemporary of William Blake. Gillray's robust draughtsmanship led him to satirical engraving, in which he drew on the tradition of Hogarth but introduced

Social satire
(above) In Gillray's cartoon, Edward Jenner is shown using his vaccine against small pox. Cows erupt from the bodies of the patients – a reference to the belief that, because the vaccine was distilled from cow pox, recipients would develop the characteristics of cattle.

Max Beckmann (1884-1950)

Leading German Expressionist painter. Beckmann studied at the Weimar Academy and visited Paris and Geneva before settling in Berlin, where he joined the Sezession. During the War, he was invalided out of the army after suffering a nervous breakdown and this traumatic period influenced his violent, hallucinatory style. Through the latter, he formed a link between the mainstream of German Expressionism and the Neue Sachlichkeit practised by Grosz and Dix. Beckmann's work was included in the Nazis' exhibition of 'Degenerate Art' (1937) and, accordingly, he moved to Holland. In 1947, he went to America where he taught for a time at Washington University, St Louis, before his death in New York.

George Cruikshank (1792-1878)

English painter and caricaturist. George was taught to etch by his father, Isaac, but his work owed a greater debt to the example of Gillray. Cruikshank completed a number of the latter's unfinished plates and continued his tirades against Napoleon and the Prince Regent. However, during Queen Victoria's reign, the taste for hard-hitting political satire subsided and Cruikshank turned to less provocative, social issues. His best-known works in this vein were his designs for The Bottle (1847), which formed part of the Temperance campaign.

Honoré Daumier (1808-79)

French painter, sculptor and lithographer. Daumier first came to notice as a political caricaturist, and in 1832 he was imprisoned for representing King Louis-Philippe as the gluttonous Gargantua. Caricature, the journal in

140

an unbridled ferocity that was all his own. He did not solely attack political figures – George III and Napoleon were his favourite targets – but also lampooned the latest social trends. Gillray's work enjoyed great popular success and there was a certain kudos to be gained from becoming the butt of his humour. Sadly, his career was curtailed by fits of insanity.

Jean-François Millet (1814-75)
French painter, associated with the Realist movement. Millet was born of peasant stock and studied initially in Cherbourg, before completing his training in Paris under Delaroche. His early work consisted mainly of portraits and nudes until, in the late 1840s, he turned to the large-scale peasant scenes with which his name is now irrevocably linked. To modern eyes, these pictures now appear essentially Romantic and occasionally sentimental. However, in the aftermath of the 1848 Revolution, they seemed charged with political intent and, as a result, Millet was swept up in the Realist controversy. His own views are uncertain, and in 1849 he settled permanently in Barbizon, where he continued to paint peasant subjects and landscapes. The moral undertones of his work proved an influence on Van Gogh.

William Morris (1834-96)
English writer and painter, a pioneer of the Arts and Crafts movement. Morris studied at Oxford University, where he met Burne-Jones. Together, they belonged to the second generation of Pre-Raphaelite artists and assisted Rossetti in the execution of the Oxford Union murals. Morris trained as an architect, but his true vocation lay in the applied arts. His firm, Morris & Company (founded in 1861), produced a wide range of designs for furniture, stained-glass and wallpaper, and provided a vital stimulus for the development of the Arts and Crafts movement. He also attempted to raise the standards of book production through the foundation in 1890 of the Kelmscott Press, the most famous of the English private presses. Morris was a dedicated socialist and, in his writings, he preached the superiority of hand-made over mass-produced goods.

José Clemente Orozco (1883-1949)
Mexican mural painter. Orozco's early career was divided between graphic work for journals and paintings illustrating the poverty of pre-Revolutionary Mexican life. In 1922, he executed his first large-scale pictures, as part of the murals commissioned for the National Preparatory School, and between 1927-34 he produced further mural designs in the United States, most notably those at Pomona College, California, and Dartmouth College, New Hampshire. Orozco's interests were humanitarian rather than political, but his style could achieve a genuine heroic grandeur, as in the magnificent murals at the Instituto Cabanas, in Guadalajara (1939).

Thomas Rowlandson (1756-1827)
English watercolourist and caricaturist. Rowlandson was born in London, the son of a silk merchant. He entered the Royal Academy Schools in 1772 and completed his training in Paris. On his return, he exhibited at the Academy, winning a silver medal in 1777. However, his reputation was forged by his abundant drawing and smaller watercolours. In these, he married a Rococo lightness of touch with the earthiest of subject-matter, covering the full gamut of English social life. Rowlandson worked in a bawdy and humorous manner that owed much to the example of Hogarth, although it lacked the latter's moralizing tone. Indeed, his own lifestyle mirrored the ebullience of his pictures, many of which were produced as payments for his frequent gambling debts.

John Ruskin (1819-1900)
Influential English writer and artist. Ruskin was brought up near London, the son of a prosperous sherry merchant, and his precocious literary talent was coloured by the strict, evangelical leanings of his parents. In 1840, he met Turner and championed his achievements in the first volume of his Modern Painters (1843). In subsequent writings, he gave evidence of a very personal aesthetic – highlighted by his support for the Pre-Raphaelites and for the Gothic style, and by his distaste for both Classical and Baroque painting – which was fuelled by a strong, moral commitment. These beliefs drew him into the infamous libel case with Whistler, the cause célèbre of the Aesthetic movement. In addition to his writing, Ruskin was a gifted watercolourist and draughtsman, producing many precise and lyrical studies of nature. His personal life, however, was a disaster. His wife, Effie, left him to marry Millais and he suffered from mental illness in his final years.

David Alfaro Siqueiros (1896-1974)
Mexican painter and activist. In his youth, Siqueiros travelled widely in Europe, making contact with avant-garde circles and confirming his own Marxist tendencies. On his return home, in 1922, he founded the Syndicate of Technical Workers, Painters and Sculptors and, soon after, he collaborated with Rivera and Orozco on the new murals for the National Preparatory School. Siqueiros' own vigorous style was influenced both by Mexican folk art and by Surrealism, and was notable for its technical innovations (such as using silicates in place of pigments). During his exile in the USA, he founded the Experimental Workshop in New York (1936).

Political satire
(left) Daumier is generally considered to be the father-figure of modern caricature. In this dramatic composition, the skeletal figure of Death thanks the German Chancellor Bismark for all the wars he has caused.

141

INDEX